START WITH STORY

LYN GRAFT

START

WITH

STORY

THE ENTREPRENEUR'S GUIDE TO USING
STORY TO **GROW YOUR BUSINESS**

LIONCREST
PUBLISHING

START WITH STORY

The Entrepreneur's Guide to Using Story to Grow Your Business

ISBN   978-1-5445-0139-0 *Paperback*
          978-1-5445-0138-3 *Ebook*

To my mom, Eva Graft, the North Star of my life
and the best storyteller I've ever known.

To my sisters, Cindy, Lindy, Mindy, and Windy.
Why, I'm the luckiest brother in the world.

To my four-legged best friend, Fitty G. Best.
Dog. Ever. You broke the mold for dogs.

To my two-legged best friend, Ingrid Vanderveldt
"iV." Thank you for always being there.

And to all those who believed in me. You rock. #TrueStory

CONTENTS

INTRODUCTION

I WAS TIRED, FRUSTRATED, AND CONFUSED ABOUT what to do next. Two years after I finished my MBA at the University of Texas at Austin, I began my first start-up, a tech company with my best friend. We were months into the launch and were readying to approach angel investors for our first outside investment.

We had been working on our business plan and pitch deck for months and had been told by peers and informal advisors that there were still umpteen things wrong even after all the updates and changes we'd made. She and I felt completely lost. It was late afternoon on a Monday when I remembered a monthly meeting that night at the Austin Software Council where they would be bringing in a speaker to talk all things start-up. We were still chipping away at our deck, and I had originally planned to skip the talk because we had too much to do. There was no time to listen to someone yammer on about their start-up when ours needed so much work.

However, completely drained by the current challenge, I decided to get out of my apartment and step away from my computer to take a break from the grind. I arrived late to the meeting and had no clue who the speaker was, but the two-hundred-seat auditorium was packed. I assumed the guy was important but didn't recognize him as he stood at the podium.

He carried a duffle bag to the podium and began by stating that he'd like to tell his story using a set of T-shirts he had in the duffle bag. He reached over and pulled out a T-shirt with a company logo on it. He held it up for everyone to see and said, "This was my first company."

I had never heard the company name or seen the logo before. "This was a cool idea," he said, "but we never could get the technology to work." He put that shirt down, reached into the duffle bag, and pulled out another shirt. Again, unrecognizable. "Now, this company was a cool idea," he began. "We got it to work, but we couldn't turn it into a product that anybody cared about, so that company failed as well." He put that shirt down and pulled out another. "This was our third company. It was a great idea and great technology. We turned it into a product that worked, but nobody would buy it. It was a terribly frustrating situation." He shook his head, put that shirt down, and pulled out yet another. "This company was a great idea, great technology, and a great product. We started selling, but a key partner didn't want the product to continue, so we ended up shutting it down."

He put that T-shirt back in the bag, and at this point, I remember thinking, *This man has failed multiple times, and he's confidently sharing his failures; he has to be someone special.* He went on to share another failure. From what I recall, this was another great idea, great company, great team, incredible technology, product, and market opportunity, but it was just the wrong timing. They lost millions of their investors' money. At this point, I was thinking, *Who is this guy?*

Finally, he held up his last T-shirt but kept the name on it hidden. Then he said, "This was a great company. Great idea, great technology, great market opportunity, great founding team. And the people that had just lost the money in our previous company? They funded us."

He turned the shirt around, and in big letters on the front, it said AOL.

AOL, or America Online Inc., was one of the most successful and recognized web brands in the 1990s and an early pioneer of the internet. The man on the stage that night was Marc Seriff, one of the original founders.

That night, I went home with a new sense of optimism and vigor to complete the deck and business plan. The work paid off. Within a few weeks, we closed our first $100,000 seed investment. The company I founded would go on to have its own ups and downs, but what remained from that experience that night was Marc Seriff's story and the inspiration it gave me.

When I spoke to Marc recently, I told him how he'd inspired me. He was humbly honored. Though I may not have remembered the exact dialogue or all the exact details of his story, the spirit of what Marc said and the message of perseverance and determination were the same. All these years later, I can still picture Marc on stage with his duffle bag and T-shirts. I remember exactly what I felt, what I saw, and how it motivated me. I didn't know it at the time, but that talk planted the entrepreneurial storytelling seed in me, and I would soon come to learn how powerful story can be.

THE ENTREPRENEUR'S JOURNEY

Entrepreneurship is one of the most rewarding and fulfilling endeavors you can undertake. Few things give you the kind of personal pride and internal reverence that comes with being called a founder, where every decision starts with you—from the company name to the culture to the product you want to build or service you provide.

At the same time, few things are more all-consuming than launching a company. You are often operating on an island, responsible for everything with no one to turn to. You alone are the champion of your idea. No one has ever heard of your business or knows who you are or what your product does. You work with few resources on a limited runway, constantly punching above your weight class.

To compete as a start-up, you need something that levels the playing field. You need something that allows you to compete no matter the time, place, setting, or resources. You need an instrument of persuasion and influence that gives you an advantage over market gorillas one hundred times your size.

That instrument is your story.

Twenty years after hearing Marc Seriff's story, the lesson remains the same: a great story changes everything. A compelling story has the power to catalyze movements, disrupt industries, and topple giants. It can help build empires, create legends, and rewrite history. Almost every successful entrepreneur started his or her company with a story. And every founder can create a great story—regardless of industry, age, or resources. The more you invest in story, the more it will help you accomplish your goals. In fact, there is a direct correlation between success and the entrepreneur's ability to create and tell their founding story.

Blake Mycoskie, the founder of TOMS, knows this well. One day, Blake was in an airport and saw a woman wearing a pair of the shoes he'd designed and manufactured. Without identifying himself, he told her, "I really like your shoes." The woman turned to him and said, "Oh, these shoes are amazing. The company that sells these shoes is incredible. For every pair that gets bought, a child in need in another country gets an equal pair of shoes. It's truly amazing."

He kind of smiled to himself and said, "That's great," and started walking away.

The woman reached over his shoulder, grabbed him, and said, louder and with more emotion, "No, you don't understand; for every pair of shoes that a person buys, a child in need, a person in need, gets a free pair of shoes. That's unbelievable."

She was so passionate about the idea that Blake realized something exceptionally powerful that day. The very product, the very thing that he was selling, was a story;

and because of that story, his customers had become his evangelists. Once an audience understands an idea like Blake Mycoskie's—that for every pair of shoes that you buy, someone else in another country who has no money is going to get a pair of shoes—they will forever be tied to that association.

That's the real power of the story—to create an immeasurable connection between you and your audience. Connection is the magic that makes stories work, more so than any fact or figure you could ever share. Story is one of those rare tools that simultaneously connects us yet allows us to distinguish ourselves by bringing to light our uniqueness.

DISCOVERING THE POWER OF STORY

As an entrepreneur who's spent the last fifteen years filming entrepreneurs like Blake Mycoskie for a living, I know firsthand how powerful story is. My production company is responsible for capturing and sharing the stories of entrepreneurs worldwide. I've produced videos for TV networks, magazines, and corporations as well as for the founders themselves. I've even created and produced a series for CNBC called *American Made*. I have the good fortune to be around the best of the best, having filmed more than five hundred of the top entrepreneurs in the world, including the founders of Starbucks, Whole

Foods, LinkedIn, Paul Mitchell, Dropbox, Zappos, and The Knot.

But before I delved into producing videos, I was a founder looking for ways to bring my ideas to life and figuring out how to get the resources I needed to build companies around them. I've been told no by dozens of media outlets, hundreds of investors, and thousands of prospects. I've started eight companies and organizations, crashed and burned miserably a few times, and had some good fortune in others. My path has been varied. I have dabbled in everything from a high-tech start-up to e-commerce to a nonprofit to a production company. You could say I'm a "dyed-in-the-wool entrepreneur."

Yet despite my many setbacks, whether consciously or not, through story I've been able to get my start-ups featured in the *Wall Street Journal, Inc.* magazine, and the *New York Times*, raise $10 million in venture capital, and generate millions in revenue over the last two decades. During my years as a founder and subsequent journey filming top entrepreneurs, I discovered something incredibly profound.

Your story is your power.

Story runs through the very fabric of everything we do as entrepreneurs, whether we realize it or not. It is used in every facet of the business—from getting press, to fund-raising, to closing sales, to recruiting people to work for you for free, to getting a partner to help you launch a start-up or convincing your spouse to let you take out all the savings to chase your dream. Once I understood the sheer scope and jaw-dropping power of a founder's story, my mission became clear to me—to help other entrepreneurs discover their own unique story so they could use it to be successful.

I also recognized that there is not a single person on this planet who has had the same unique experiences and direct access that I have had to some of the world's best entrepreneurs. Now, through this book and its corresponding online course on my Storytelling for Entrepreneurs website, I can channel that experience and knowledge to help founders like you learn about the art and science of entrepreneurial storytelling.

Within this book, you are going to find dozens of examples of how some of the most successful entrepreneurs on the planet leveraged their story to launch and grow their companies. I will share stories of entrepreneurs like the founders of Dropbox, Pandora, and Starbucks so you can learn from the best of the best.

I'm going to deconstruct a story into parts that you can understand and leverage as you see fit. I will show you how to craft a story that grabs the attention of your audience, makes a connection, and ultimately motivates them to take an action in your favor.

I will share a straightforward, easy-to-learn, and fast-to-implement method to help you create your founding story—a story that you can use indefinitely to grow and succeed. You will learn how to distinguish between your business needs and your story goals and how to leverage the experiences that put you on this entrepreneurial journey into a story that mesmerizes every person you meet.

Part of my passion for entrepreneurial storytelling comes from my first ever "paid" video production gig fifteen years ago. Through a series of synergistic events, I had the opportunity to film and interview three billionaire entrepreneurs who had created three of the top corporations in the country: Michael Dell (founder of Dell Computers), Red McCombs (founder of Clear Channel), and Dr. George Kozmetsky (one of Texas's first billionaires and the founder of Teledyne). These founders all came from very different backgrounds, with different personalities, and they all had a unique way of sharing their story and imparting pearls of wisdom about success in business. I was mesmerized.

I left the set with a buzzing feeling—like I had to share

the story with my mom, or sister, or best friend, or colleague who had just started a similar business. I saw (and felt) the value in these stories, but I also realized that so many entrepreneurs didn't appreciate the value of their own story.

As an entrepreneur, you might not think that you or your business is that interesting, but trust me...you are. The fact that you started your own company is amazing, and if you can learn to tap into your special story, then you can use that to your advantage in every situation.

YOUR GREATEST TOOL

As a founder, you are going to be given countless opportunities to share your story in front of every audience you can imagine. A good story is the Swiss Army knife of entrepreneurship—available to tackle any problem. You will use story for every facet of your business and throughout the entire life of your company. Story allows you to share your gift with the world in a way that moves people to want to help you. And it gives you the power to leverage everything that is singularly unique about you and to turn it into a competitive advantage.

Story is one of the greatest tools you have as an entrepreneur. And remember this: every good product is one great story away from being a business success. All you have to do is create it and watch what it can do for you. As Phil Knight, the founder of Nike, once said:

"Any building is a temple if you make it so."

It's time to make your building that temple. Starting with story is the first step.

Let's begin.

CHAPTER ONE

THE POWER OF STORY

STORIES ARE ONE OF THE MOST POWERFUL FORCES on the planet. As humans, story is part of who we are. We have been immersed in storytelling since we began walking the earth. Anthropologists have found evidence of stories in every culture and society on the planet. They can be found in cave drawings, scrolls, paintings, and religion. History itself is filled with stories—from Hercules to King Arthur, Julius Caesar to Plato, and Athena to Cleopatra.

Before the written word, men, women, and children sat around the fire telling tales to entertain and transfer wisdom from the old to the young. The act of storytelling was a way for mankind to protect the clan and survive. It kept us from danger, told us where to grow crops, and told us where to find food and water. It created community, bringing together the tribe around the campfire after the day was done. Story is part of our ethos. No matter where you're from, who you are, or your ethnicity, gender, or socioeconomic background, you are exposed to story.

STORY AND OUR DNA

From birth to death, storytelling permeates every stage of our lives. From the moment we're born, we're inundated with stories. You could say they're in our DNA. When we are babies, before we even understand words or language, our parents read stories to us. As we grow, stories are ingrained in our education and life experiences. Whether those stories come through school, church, books, TV shows, games, or movies, they are always there. From *Charlotte's Web* to *Moby Dick*, from Greek mythology to *Star Wars*, as well as the tales our grandparents and parents tell, story is how we are entertained, how we learn, and how we make sense of the world.

Stories are woven into every aspect of our personal and professional lives. We grow up with stories like David versus Goliath or The Little Engine That Could and learn we can accomplish anything, no matter our stature. When we enter the business world, we turn to luminaries like Henry Ford, John D. Rockefeller, Mary Kay Ash, or Walt Disney for the same kind of inspiration.

In the last few decades, entrepreneurs have become the

fabled heroes we long to read about. Whereas the stories of the iconic and incredible used to focus on literary characters and mythological figures, or presidents and generals, they are now focused on people like Richard Branson and Elon Musk, Oprah Winfrey and Martha Stewart. We learn about success in business through the stories of the great entrepreneurs of the world. We're inspired by their teachings and journeys because we're naturally inclined to absorb and gravitate toward good stories.

In fact, we are biologically wired to interpret life through stories.

THE SCIENCE OF STORIES

Stories go beyond bedtime reading and lessons in school—they are part of the physical and chemical makeup of human comprehension. Stories are not only part of our DNA and our ethos, but they also trigger physical reactions within the human body.

The simple act of telling a story activates more parts of the brain in an audience than just numbers or stats, thus creating a higher probability of connection between the speaker and the audience. A fact triggers two parts of the brain to become more active, while a compelling story can cause six to seven parts of the brain to become more active.[1] On top of this, you are six times more likely to remember the information contained within a story than you are to remember a fact or figure on its own.[2]

When more parts of the brain become more active, chemicals are released, creating a similar reaction in the body as other stimulating activities. The same chemicals that release when you eat chocolate, have sex, or do drugs are released when you hear a story. These chemicals that are triggered in the brain and sent throughout the body make you feel good when you hear a great story, sad when you hear a depressing story, or excited when someone's elated.

I talked with Dr. Paul Zak, founding director of the Center for Neuroeconomics Studies and professor of economics, psychology, and management at Claremont Graduate University, to get a better understanding of what happens when these neurochemicals are released in the brain. As a neuroscientist, Dr. Zak does extensive work studying neurochemicals to help quantify the impact of stories, movies, and advertising on consumer experiences. He is credited with the discovery of the behavioral effect

---

1   Alexander G. Huth et al., "Natural Speech Reveals the Semantic Maps That Tile Human Cerebral Cortex," *Nature* 532 (2016): 453–58, https://www.nature.com/articles/nature17637; J. González et al., "Reading Cinnamon Activates Olfactory Brain Regions," *Neoroimage* 32, no. 2 (2006): 906–12, https://www.ncbi.nlm.nih.gov/pubmed/16651007.

2   G. H. Bower and M. C. Clark, "Narrative Stories as Mediators for Serial Learning," *Psychonomic Science* 14 (1969): 181–82.

of oxytocin (often called the love hormone), a neuro-chemical in the brain that motivates people to engage in cooperative behaviors. In his studies, he has found that compelling stories that trigger oxytocin have the power to affect our attitudes, beliefs, and behaviors.

Dr. Zak shared that these neurochemicals are a driving factor in why stories can stimulate higher levels of attention from audiences and forge an emotional connection with them. When we are exposed to an immersive story, a series of chemicals, such as ACTH and cortisol, which are arousal neurochemicals, cause the brain to pay attention. Subsequently, oxytocin, referred to as the love chemical because it triggers emotions such as kindness and empathy, is also released, which creates a level of trust. When you hear a compelling story, this combination of chemicals creates a compounding effect, causing you to pay attention and care about the characters and purpose of the story. Dr. Zak adds, "When you're emotionally engaged in the story, your brain produces chemicals that allow you to begin to share the emotions of the story you are listening to."

This neurochemical reaction is why when you read a book or watch a movie you feel your blood pumping through your body. That same chemical reaction also explains why you feel sad and cry with the characters or happily laugh along with them. Even though you know cognitively that what you are reading or viewing is not real, you still feel as if you are experiencing every aspect of the story being presented. This is called the Mirror Effect.[3] The Mirror Effect says that whatever experience the story gives is that which the audience will literally experience. The same thing happens when you're in front of a person and you're telling a good story. Their brain will mimic what's happening in your brain.

A study done by Professor Uri Hasson at Princeton demonstrated exactly this. Professor Hasson is a neuroscience professor who studied the effect of story on the brain. For his experiment, he had a woman tell a story in English, then tell the same story in Russian. Her brain was monitored, as were the people's brains in the audience. All the listeners only understood English, not Russian. When she shared the story in English, they all understood her story and their brains started syncing with hers. The thought and emotion areas of the brain—the insula, the frontal cortex, and a variety of other areas—started mimicking what was going on in her brain. The more the audience understood the story, the more their brain patterns and responses matched hers. When the woman went back and read the story in Russian, with the same inflection points and the same emotional delivery, the audience's brains had zero corresponding activity,

3   Giorgio Coricelli, "Two-Levels of Mental States Attribution: From Automaticity to Voluntariness," *Neuropsychologia* 43, no. 2 (2005): 294–300.

because they didn't comprehend what she was saying. Since they didn't understand what was being said, there was no story being shared. Therefore, there was no connection, because the brain was not activated.[4]

When you can create a physiological response through story, it has incredible power.

Maya Angelou famously stated, "They may not remember what you did for them or what you said, but they will remember how you made them feel." That is the secret sauce in any story. It's this feeling, this *je ne sais quoi*, that speaks to the association that you have with a great story. It is the heart.

The heart is where the connection is made with the audience—preparing them mentally, emotionally, psychologically, and spiritually for however you want them to feel. When the heartstrings are pulled, the audience will follow wherever you lead them.

Stories that cause us to pay attention and involve us emotionally are the stories that move us to action.

---

4   Christopher J. Honey et al., "Not Lost in Translation: Neural Responses Shared across Languages," *Journal of Neuroscience* 32, no. 44 (2012): 15277–83.

EMOTIONAL DECISIONS

As entrepreneurs, we are constantly looking for ways to talk about our business so that people make a decision in our favor. We want them to buy our product, invest, write about us, take a meeting, or come work with us. We are trying to influence these decisions because the responses have a tremendous impact on our daily success. And alternatively, people don't make decisions based on facts and information—they make decisions based on emotion. A story can persuade an audience to decide in your favor because it's infused with emotion. We tend to believe that the choices we make are a result of a rational analysis of the facts and available alternatives. However, research has shown that decision-making isn't logical at all; it's emotional.

Antonio Damasio, a professor of neuroscience at the University of Southern California, purports in his book *Descartes' Error* that emotion is a key ingredient in decision-making. In 1982, Damasio had a patient named Elliot with a brain tumor, which he subsequently removed. Though the operation was deemed a success and Elliot still scored in the 97th IQ percentile, Elliot's life began to fall apart. He lacked all motivation and could not make decisions. He would endlessly debate over trivial things in his life. Damasio realized that the tumor had been located in the part of the brain responsible for emotion.

In following Elliot's progress, he discovered that when the

area of the brain responsible for generating emotions was damaged, the patient was unable to make decisions even if the rest of the brain functioned normally. The logical, undamaged part of the brain allowed Elliot to perform everyday tasks, but he couldn't decide simple things, such as where to eat or what to wear. He could rationally process information about choices, but he was unable to make decisions, because he did not have a "feeling" about the options before him. Damasio discovered that emotion ultimately drives us to action. Without emotion, humans are not compelled to act, regardless of a situation's importance or how much information is provided.

To paraphrase Dr. Damasio, appealing to the heart is more effective than appealing to the head. If you focus on developing a great story, you'll have a higher probability of reaching someone emotionally. And humans act from emotion. Emotions have the power to inspire and motivate. They communicate the passion behind an idea or belief and aid in discerning what matters. Evoking an emotional reaction from your audience helps them understand why they should care. The emotion makes them want to listen to your idea and understand where it fits into their life and how it affects them.

Weaving a message into a compelling story is one of the most effective methods to reach, influence, and persuade an audience. Stories can disrupt and even change the most deeply held prejudices and beliefs. If you can move people with a narrative that conveys your idea emotionally, there's a good chance they will embrace it on a gut level. If created and told effectively, stories convey a message to the audience that the conditions are optimal for them to make a decision. Whether it's asking for funding or press, a sale or a partnership, stories trigger the brain into responding in a favorable manner.

For entrepreneurs, a great story can be the tool that changes your entire world.

THE SWISS ARMY KNIFE OF ENTREPRENEURSHIP

One of the primary reasons to have a story as an entrepreneur is that often it's the only thing you possess. Some founders may start out with a team of people, have secured funding before launching, or even have some form of brand recognition, but the reality is that for 99 percent of all business owners out there, it's just you and an idea when you first begin. Like the majority of entrepreneurs, you have close to nothing, yet you must do everything.

Story is the one asset that can be created right now without resources, providing you with a powerful tool to help you secure the resources you lack. Like a Swiss Army knife, story can be used for every business need—raising capital, driving sales, developing partnerships, getting press, and recruiting. Story makes the intangible tangible, the mundane magnificent, the impossible fathomable. It creates an emotional bridge between you and your audience. As a founder, a story connects you to everything you need.

Peter Guber, a revered Hollywood producer whose films have earned more than $3 billion worldwide and garnered fifty Academy Award nominations, talks extensively about this idea in his book *Tell to Win: Connect, Persuade, and Triumph with the Hidden Power of Story*. One of the core premises of Peter's book is that stories are your Trojan horse.

Like the horse, stories are a gift to the audience and a means of delivery. They get the message past the defensive walls of the audience. Right now, we are flooded with more information than at any other time in history. We are constantly bombarded by ads, sales pitches, and social media. Because of this increase of information, we automatically throw up guards, both consciously and subconsciously. We are more selective about the information we choose to receive, and tune out that which we do not care to hear.

As business owners, we must look for ways to break through the chatter of our tech-enhanced world and grab people's attention. A story can do just that by lowering people's guard. With a story, your message gets subconsciously embedded in the listener because they're interested, relating, learning, or caring about what is being said. They have crossed the bridge and are in the story with you, just like the subjects of Hasson's experiment on the Mirror Effect. By the time they've finished listening to the story, they feel a certain way about the business, the product, or the service and will often take action without having to be persuaded to do so.

FOUNDER'S STORY: BERT JACOBS

The story of Bert Jacobs, one of the founders of Life Is Good, exemplifies how the power of a story can change everything. I saw Bert Jacobs speak and met him at the Texas for Women Conference a few years back when he was on his book tour. I experienced the passion, impact, and raw emotion of Bert's transcendent storytelling power firsthand during his speech and my subsequent conversations with him.

Bert and his five siblings grew up in a lower-middle-class family in Massachusetts. Their house was small and chaotic. They may not have had much, but their parents taught them what mattered most in life—friends, family, laughter, and love. Their father was a craftsman and the breadwinner for the entire family. One day, Bert's father was in a car accident that almost killed him. While he survived, the injuries from the accident ruined the use of his right arm, which effectively destroyed his career and led him to sink into a deep depression with volatile mood swings.

Bert's mother, determined not to let the accident affect the family, worked hard to make sure the kids always looked for the positive in life. Every night at dinner, if things turned bad, she used a simple trick to change their mood. She would look around the table and say, "Tell me something good that happened today," and the kids would each share their experiences. Bert observed how the energy around the table would instantly change. Everyone would end up laughing together. This small act of infusing optimism was a lesson that would serve him well for years to come.

When the boys graduated college, they wanted to travel, so they took odd jobs. One of the brothers went to California to teach, and another went to Colorado to become a ski instructor. On one of their road trips to visit each other, they decided to start a business together. They looked at their combined skillset—one was good with graphic design and the other was good with words—and started a T-shirt company.

They went back to Massachusetts, bought a van from one of the other brothers, who worked in the used-car industry, and went to work. They spent their entire savings, which at the time was around $160, and bought their first set of T-shirts. For the next five years, they traveled up and down the East Coast, selling T-shirts at festivals and universities, making a buck wherever they could. But they never made much money. In fact, they were working part-time as school teachers in the local elementary and high schools to pay the bills, and sometimes they would sleep at the dormitories at the universities to avoid having to spend money on hotels.

Despite not having much money, they always had a good outlook on life and great conversations. On the return from one of their long road trips to a festival where they'd sold shirts, they started talking about how the news was pessimistic—constantly telling people what was wrong with the world and preying on people's fears. Bert and his brother began reminiscing on how their mom used to always ask about the good things in their lives. They started thinking that maybe they should do something with their business to add more optimism to life.

When they returned to their apartment in Boston, they invited all their friends over to work on new ideas. This was their tradition. They'd get a keg, start drinking, and everyone would contribute by drawing their ideas on the apartment walls. They told everyone their idea about adding optimism to life and told them to have at it. That night, many great characters and sayings ended up on the walls, but one stood out: a beret-wearing smiley face with sunglasses on. Next to it were the words "This guy's got it figured out."

They loved how he looked, and after the party, they worked on that sketch and came up with a simple three-word saying: "Life is good." They decided to take the last bit of money they had, seventy-eight dollars, and make forty-eight T-shirts. They went to downtown Boston and sold all forty-eight shirts in forty-five minutes. They made more in that forty-five minutes than they typically made in a week.

In that moment, they knew they not only had a great idea for a shirt, but they also had the beginnings of something far more than a slogan and a drawing. They had a story—a story that captured the spirit of optimism that their mother had implanted in them as children. It was an ideal that represented an optimistic view about the good in the world. They went from being two guys living in a van for five years, making no money, to having their lives changed overnight because they captured their idea in a three-word slogan and a sunglass-wearing stick figure on a T-shirt.

The magic of their story is that they took the optimism they grew up with and turned it into a slogan and a company that represented everything positive they believed in. Their story literally changed everything for them that day. Bert and his brother went on to turn that story and that vision into what is now a hundred-million-dollar company, available in forty-five hundred retailers in all fifty states, and thirty countries. Now, everywhere you go, you can find "Life is good" and that smiley-faced spirit on everything they create.

CHAPTER TWO

WHAT IS A STORY?

ACCORDING TO WEBSTER'S DICTIONARY, STORY IS "an account of incidences or events. It's a statement regarding the facts pertinent to a situation in question." While this is true, story is so much more. If you study story, you can get lost quickly in the details of what constitutes one. However, as an entrepreneur, you don't need to know the complex definitions and plethora of terminology of story. As an entrepreneur, all you need to know is that the vast majority of great entrepreneurial storytellers are successful because they can relate their business or vision to something that has a strong meaning in their life. In that connection lies the secret to the entrepreneurial story.

STORY IS AN EXPERIENCE

When I began my career filming and capturing stories of

entrepreneurs, I was a novice to the craft. My engineering, MBA, and start-up background didn't exactly prepare me for filming founders and creating narrative stories for video or television, and I had to rely on pure gut instinct. Luckily, I was able to leverage the skills of the other producers, camera operators, and video editors I worked with, who were good writers and storytellers themselves.

As I produced more videos featuring founders, I became better at capturing and telling their stories in a concise and compelling manner. I continued filming well-known founders of fast-growth start-ups and large corporations, and soon business organizations and corporations began asking me to speak about entrepreneurial storytelling at their meetings and events. Simultaneously, entrepreneurs asked me if I could help them with their story. Since I was going to be teaching others about it, I figured it was time to go deep and learn about the brass tacks of story and storytelling.

Hence, I dove into the history of story and discovered how the Greeks and the Romans came up with two-, three-, and four-part structures for plays. Then I heard about a famous German playwright named Gustav Freytag, who developed the dramatic arc that soon became all the rage in the 1800s. I began reading books on the subject of story, talked to writers, and researched the work of well-known film and narrative structure experts Robert McKee and

Joseph Campbell. I learned terms like denouement and apotheosis, structures that needed to be followed, and character categorizations that had to be developed.

Though this deep dive was fascinating, it confused and frustrated me. I wasn't trying to write a Pulitzer Prize-winning book or make a blockbuster movie. I simply wanted to create and share inspiring stories about entrepreneurs. Why did I need characters when I was trying to explain to someone why I came up with an idea for a great product? Why did there have to be a hero that went through a thirteen-stage journey of finding himself when I was simply trying to solve a problem I saw as irritating? And why did I have to know how to use a denouement when I couldn't pronounce it nor even knew what it meant? (By the way, denouement means the climax of a chain of events, usually when something is decided or made clear, and it's pronounced 'dānōō'mäN.)

From my perspective, the complex structures inherent in great storytelling in books, movies, and manuscripts weren't designed with a business owner in mind. These structures were typically created for people working in entertainment or publishing, where their job is to create movies, plays, and books that can hold an audience's attention for a long period of time. Or they were made for marketing departments and advertising agencies with massive resources who wanted to create comprehensive ad campaigns.

Most people, especially entrepreneurs, don't care about the climax or the hero and the shadow figure, because we don't talk like that, nor do we understand what those terms mean or how they relate to our business (nor do we care, for that matter). The entrepreneurial story is short and to the point. It's not a grand opus, nor a Star Wars trilogy, nor a multiweek, six-month advertising campaign on Madison Avenue.

Entrepreneurs talk about the inspiration for the business or the epiphany we had in the middle of the night. Great entrepreneurs talk about how they came up with an idea that led to the biggest coffee business in the world or the catalyst that enabled them to build to a hundred-million-dollar T-shirt business. They talk about their trials and their triumphs, and they make it feel natural.

I asked a number of successful entrepreneurs I'd filmed how they came up with their founding story and how it evolved over time. I even inquired if they'd studied story structure or knew what any of these terms meant. Almost no one had studied this subject or returned to learn about this topic. They figured it out on their own. So I decided to start from scratch and learn entrepreneurial storytelling from those who knew better than anyone else—the entrepreneurs themselves.

I rewatched the videos I had produced featuring big-name entrepreneurs and reviewed countless transcripts of our interviews. I thought about the most memorable talks I had seen entrepreneurs give in graduate school, speeches I'd seen at conferences, and the numerous times I'd spent multiple days with entrepreneurs filming their stories. I reflected on the times I'd been able to sit in a room with founders over dinner or drinks and have intimate discussions and extended talks. I sifted through autobiographies I collected on the founders I admired most and read hundreds of articles saved from the ones I'd been studying. I remembered the way these entrepreneurs told me how they started their company, what led to their idea, or the aha moment that changed everything. I loved their stories, but I couldn't put my finger on what they were doing or saying from a story-structure perspective that made them so compelling, simple, and natural...but soon it became clear.

They weren't using a complicated formula; *they were all sharing experiences.*

I was awestruck. *How could it be that simple?* But it was. It didn't matter the industry—whether it was a product or service—and it didn't matter their age or their background; there was one common denominator between each entrepreneur. Every one of them was sharing an experience they'd had.

They simply crafted their story around an experience that pertained to their company and became better and better at telling it through trial and error. To a certain degree, sharing an experience was something I had been doing my entire life. I often start stories with my friends and colleagues with "Do you remember that time..." I don't think about my story in terms of a twelve-step process or speak in terms they don't understand. I simply recall an experience that has relevance to the conversation and share that experience in such a way that it brings them into it emotionally. This is the cornerstone of entrepreneurial storytelling.

The real beauty of this discovery is the elegance in its simplicity:

STORY = EXPERIENCE + BUSINESS MEANING

Every single one of you reading this book has a meaningful experience that relates to your business. As an entrepreneur, something inspired you to take action, build a product or create a service, and found a company. There's a reason you became a business owner, and inevitably there's an experience that put you on the path of being a founder. That experience could be a problem that you encountered that you had to solve. It could be a major failure or setback in your life that you wanted to do something about. It could be an epiphany that you had in the shower or a revelation you had when you were out for a run. If that experience had an impact on you, then there's a high probability that same experience is going to have an impact on someone else.

That is the beauty of storytelling for entrepreneurs. It's as simple as determining what that experience was and sharing it in the right way. Case in point, the story of Howard Schultz—my favorite entrepreneurial storyteller I've ever filmed. Let me share how his ability to impart his experience changed the entire world.

FOUNDER'S STORY: HOWARD SCHULTZ

Born in Brooklyn, New York, Howard Schultz grew up in a five-person family in a small two-bedroom unit, in a housing project with 150 families, in a building with one elevator. He never dreamed of working in business; his only dream was to get out of the projects. His family was too poor to send him to college, but luckily, he was good at sports and was offered a football scholarship to a small school in Michigan. That was his ticket out of New York.

Unfortunately, once Howard arrived at school, competition on the field was tough. Though he was a natural athlete growing up, college football was a whole other game, and he ended up not playing on the team, thus losing his scholarship. To stay in school, he took out loans and worked part-time and summer jobs. He even sold his blood at times to make ends meet. Howard worked enough to self-fund his way through school while maintaining a B average, and he became the first college graduate in his family. Following school, he worked at a ski lodge and spent hours thinking about what to do with his life but never had much inspiration or a calling, so he decided to enter a sales training program at Xerox. Turns out he was a natural-born salesman, and he became one of the top salespeople in the company. After a while, he wanted something new and went to work for a Swedish company called Hammarplast, which sold drip coffee machines among its many products. Howard worked his way up the company and rose to vice president and general manager, leading a team of salespeople. One of their number one buyers was a small company out of the Northwest. This Seattle company caught Howard's attention because it was buying so many drip machines and plastic cone filters. Like any good salesman would do, Howard decided to visit one of his top customers.

When he visited the owners of this coffee bean company, he became enamored with what they were doing. He was impressed with the company's knowledge of coffee and their views on choosing and roasting the beans. Everything about the operation spoke to Howard, and when he left Seattle, he walked away saying, "God, what a great company; what a great city. I'd love to be a part of that." A year later, he quit his job and went to work for them.

While he was there, he had an opportunity to travel to Italy to attend an international housewares show in Milan. One day he was walking the streets, enjoying a sunny, warm autumn day, when he noticed something. There were espresso bars sprinkled throughout the neighborhoods and streets. Howard had stumbled upon the coffee culture that is Italy. He saw firsthand the Italian coffee bar. These were gathering places for everyone from the community to sit around and drink espresso, cappuccino, and a myriad of coffee drinks. It was something he'd never seen in his life—an amazing, romantic, beautiful aesthetic that Italians experienced every day. Mind you, this was in 1983, and this sort of lifestyle had never been seen in the States before. Howard was immediately drawn into the romanticism of the coffee experience in Italy, and in his mind, all he could think was, *I need to bring this back to the United States.* Howard observed that the magic of these coffee bars was in the communal gathering place that they created—he coined it the "third place." We all know the first place—home—and the second place—work—but the third place was something new—a place that he needed to create in America.

After his trip, Howard returned to the coffee bean company he was working for and told the owners about his experience and how he wanted to bring it back to the United States. At the time, the company was a retailer of coffee beans, not a restaurant or a coffee shop. They thought he was crazy, but he finally convinced them to let him open a café where he would sell fresh coffee. That café was a test, and it did well, but the owners of the coffee bean company didn't want to head in that direction. Howard recognized that he wasn't going to be able to convince them to open more coffee shops, so he decided to branch out on his own. He opened a little coffee shop called Il Giornale that offered coffee and espresso beverages brewed from the coffee bean company's beans. Howard loved the name of the original coffee bean company, so he continued to buy their beans and to see if they would one day sell the name to him. One of the owners of the coffee bean company fully supported Howard, and two years later sold Howard the naming rights to their company. That company's name? Starbucks. Howard changed his company's name from Il Giornale to Starbucks and went on to build the brand we all know and love.

For Howard Schultz, the genesis of his company wasn't just about coffee or the beans. The real distinction was about creating an experience for people that emulated that third place in Italy. He wanted to build a physical location where people could experience the joy and romanticism he had experienced.

When Howard began his journey with Starbucks, he used the story of the third place experience for everything. He used it to convince his partners to let him open Il Giornale. He used it in his shop, telling customers the stories behind their coffee drinks—where they came from in Italy and why they were named what they were. He used the experience to recruit employees to work for his little old coffee shop that was going to be a national phenomenon even though he only had one store. When he went out on his own, he used it to gather partners and gain financing. The story of the third place was such a powerful vision, and magnetic, compelling idea, that Starbucks is now the most successful coffee company in the world, generating more than $16 billion a year. There are twenty-one thousand stores in sixty-five countries, and it is one of the most recognizable brands in the world, right up there with Apple, Coca-Cola, and McDonald's.

Starbucks is where it is today because Howard had the ability to share the experience he had in Italy in a way that lit people up. To this day, the reason we have coffee shops on every corner in America, and around the world for that matter, is Howard's visit to Italy and the experience of the third place. Almost single-handedly, he crafted a vision from his story that became the foundation for the coffee culture in the United States.

When we were filming Howard for *American Made*, the TV

show I produced for CNBC, the host, Ingrid Vanderveldt, asked him what we all wanted to know: "Why coffee?" Mind you, by this time we were all jonesing on caffeine because at the Starbucks headquarters there is a barista and coffee bar station on every floor, and my crew had taken full advantage of the free espressos and lattes while filming. To her question he replied, "I'm passionate about coffee and the coffee experience in the sense of community, the romance of coffee. It could have been something else, but only if I would have found something that really spoke to me." Coffee has always been at the core of Starbucks's success, but it's not the distinguishing element to their brand or story. The uniqueness of their idea was the creation of a place where people could experience the love and passion for coffee Howard had grown so fond of in Italy. It was never just about the product or service; for Howard, it was about this experience he wanted to create, where people could come and live the same thing that he saw in Europe—the third place. The power of Howard's vision for the Starbucks brand began in the story he shared of that specific experience in Italy and his ability to communicate what he felt in that moment. Though Starbucks and Howard pride themselves on their product and services, ultimately the ethos of their brand comes from this communal place re-created from that experience in Italy.

This concept is the core of what you want to do when

you create your entrepreneurial story. You want to share an experience that gets your audience to feel the same way you did, or at the very least understand the gravity of how that experience impacted you or someone you know. If you can do that, then you will have gone a long way toward getting your audience to do what you want them to do.

CHAPTER THREE

THE ENTREPRENEUR'S STORY

THE REVELATION TO UNDERSTANDING THAT AN entrepreneur's story is simply an experience was a turning point for me. It meant that I could now help anyone create a founding story regardless of their professional history, academic background, or oratory prowess. All I needed to do was provide a simple and elegant framework to go with the meaningful experience.

This is where all that time spent researching numerous academic and professional story structures, diving deep into the art and science of storytelling, and talking to hundreds of entrepreneurs came in handy.

While the structures and processes I read about didn't readily apply to the world of entrepreneurship, there were valuable ideas and important elements I could leverage to build a new framework designed specifically for entrepreneurs.

Taking inspiration from the Greek and Roman multiact play, Gustav's five-part narrative arc, and Joseph Campbell's thirteen-step hero structure, I developed a system that allows you to easily create your own story without having to understand confusing terminology or use processes with excessive steps.

Using Aristotle's model that a story simply has a beginning, a middle, and an end, and Freytag's model, which follows these three stages but breaks the beginning and the middle into two subsets to create a structure with five elements, I created an easy-to-follow framework for entrepreneurs, and it's what I'm going to teach you.

The best part is you can use this framework as the foundation for almost every story you're going to tell within your entrepreneurial life and the life of your business. It's called the Storytelling for Entrepreneurs framework or, more affectionately, SoFE—pronounced So-phie.

THE SOFE FRAMEWORK

SoFE is simple to use, easy to remember, and fast to implement. It works in any industry, with every business type, and at every stage of the business, whether it's simply an idea or a fully baked offering. Anyone can use the framework to create a story. You don't need to have a certain skill or experience to use the SoFE framework.

SoFE consists of three parts and five components. The three parts consist of a beginning, a middle, and an end. Within those three parts are five components. Two in the beginning: the setup and the incident; two in the middle: the challenge and the change; and one at the end: the outcome.

BEGINNING		MIDDLE		END
Setup	Incident	Challenge	Change	Outcome

THE BEGINNING

People often ask me what the most important part of story is. While I've heard many arguments for all aspects, I would contend that the beginning is the most important. The primary objective of the beginning is to grab the attention of the audience. If you don't grab their attention, nothing else matters. Either their attention will be lost completely, or there will be an uphill battle to gain their attention as the story continues to be told.

The beginning consists of two parts, the setup and the

incident. The setup is the background for the story, and the incident sets the narrative in motion.

The Setup

The setup gives the audience context to the story and creates a frame of reference to what is being shared. As the name implies, here the story is truly set up. The foundation is laid to prepare the audience for what's about to happen and gives them an idea as to how the story will proceed.

Let's look at an example and go back to Howard Shultz's story. What was his setup?

Howard Schultz's Starbucks story is that Howard was working for a company that made drip coffee makers, and he discovered they were selling an obscene amount of drip coffee machines to a coffee bean company in Seattle. He was impressed with their coffee knowledge, quit his job, moved to Seattle, and went to work for them. The setup is super simple, but it gives the audience enough background so that they know what's going on contextually.

The Incident

The incident is the catalyst that sets the story in motion.

This is an event, an occurrence, a big problem, a situation, or a scenario that provides the spark that ignites the fire to get the story going. The incident starts to establish a connection to the audience. The better the incident, the more it draws people into the story. When you can quickly get to this point of intrigue, your audience will want more.

Let's look at the incident in the Howard Schultz story.

While working for the Seattle coffee bean company, Howard went to visit Italy to learn more about their coffee culture. He fell in love with the communal gathering hole of the Italian coffee bar, called it the third place, and was determined to bring it back to the United States. When he references this third place in writing, videos, and especially in person, his love affair with this idea is apparent, and audiences get caught up in it. The discovery of the third place sets the tone for his story and triggers the mind to think about what he is going to do with this vision.

Or, we can take another example.

For Bert Jacobs of Life Is Good, the incident was the road trip he and his brother were on when they decided to come up with a T-shirt that helped spread the optimistic message their mother had imparted to them as kids. For Blake Mycoskie, the founder of TOMS, the incident was seeing a problem. He had witnessed numerous families without shoes and learned about a mother who had to decide which child she was going to send to school. That incident was a key moment in Blake's life that triggered decisions that would affect the rest of his life.

THE MIDDLE

Once the audience's attention is grabbed, the goal is to keep them intrigued by connecting with them. This is the middle of the story. Here, the objective is to make a connection. Since they've already been sucked in, the point now is to turn that initial suction into an industrial-scale vacuum that pulls them in like a black hole.

To do that, there are two components: the challenge and the change.

The Challenge

The challenge builds upon the connection that began in the incident and solidifies it with empathy or comprehension. When challenges are shared, people understand because everyone has suffered. We've all faced tough times, and because of that, it's easy to relate. The challenge is an obstacle that you've faced that helps build a bridge with the audience. To create a connection, the story has to matter to the audience or someone they know.

When they can see how it impacts their own life or the lives around them, they will care.

Going back to our Howard Schultz example, let's review the challenge in this story.

Howard Schultz was told he was crazy. Coffee back then was a simple necessity most Americans made at home or bought on the way to work. No one was going to care about a communal coffee shop with baristas yelling out drinks like "venti nonfat mocha latte." Yet he persisted with his idea and convinced the owners of the coffee bean company to let him open Il Giornale, that first retail coffee shop that became the physical manifestation of the Starbucks brand we love today.

The Change

Once the audience relates, they can be presented with the change. The change is the fourth component and the turning point in the story. It's a profound or climactic part of the experience that impacts everything going forward. Whether it's a solution for a problem, a resolution to a conflict, or an epiphany, the change is a core part of the experience that is recognizable and memorable. Whereas the challenge draws an audience into the experience related in the story, the change solidifies the connection with the audience.

The change in Howard Schultz's story is his deciding to go it alone after he opened that first café. For the Jacobs brothers and Life Is Good, the change is the moment in the story when they sold out of their newly designed shirts in forty-five minutes.

THE END

Once intrigue is created and a connection is made, a reaction needs to be triggered in the audience. This reaction occurs during the end, in the component called the outcome.

The Outcome

The outcome is the conclusion or resolution of the story that leaves a lasting impression. It is the culmination of everything that occurred in the beginning and the middle. It may be a decision that's been made or an action that's been taken. The purpose of the outcome is to leave the audience with some kind of feeling. Here, the goal is not to sell the audience but to leave them with a need—a "gotta have it" or "need to do something" feeling.

With this, let's review the end or outcome of the Schultz story.

When Howard Schultz shares the story about his trip to

Italy and what happened afterward, he doesn't tell you to buy his coffee or to come into his stores. He shares how he re-created the romantic experience he discovered in Italy in Starbucks stores. He tells you how he chose the finest coffee in the world and used the best techniques to make that coffee so that every time you walked into a Starbucks you experienced that third place just like he did.

By the time he finishes his story—even if you don't know about Starbucks or haven't experienced it—for most of us, his "end" creates that feeling that inspires your curiosity to at least "try" what he has created.

THE STORY'S GOAL

Great entrepreneurial storytellers rarely spend a large amount of time trying to convince their audiences to take the action they want them to take when they are sharing their story. Similar to how the best salespeople rarely have to ask for the sale, or the top start-up founders rarely have to persuade investors to put money in their deals, great entrepreneurial storytellers get things done without making their "ask" obvious. They are zeroed in on their story so much that after you hear their story you take the action they want you to take without them ever having to ask.

Have you ever been to a conference or an event where a

founder tells you their story, and before you know it, you start pulling out your smartphone to buy their book or their product, and they're not even halfway done? Or met someone who shares their story with you, and you find yourself sharing their story over and over without them ever asking you to tell anyone else? Or found yourself emailing friends and family about a company you just discovered because you want them to try their product right away? This is the goal of the story—to leave the audience with a feeling that motivates them to act.

I like to compare business need and story goal to a mousetrap. The business need is "you want the mouse gone." The cheese is the story goal. You go out and buy a mousetrap and cheese for bait. You don't buy the cheese because you want the mouse to eat it. The cheese is there to lure the mouse in. You don't tell the mouse to eat the cheese. The cheese appeals to the mouse, so they eat it on their own. If your cheese is good, then the mouse will go after it.

If the trap is any good, which is the offering, product, or service, once the mouse goes for the cheese, they're caught. The story goal is to have the mouse desire the cheese in such a way that they go after the bait.

FOUNDER'S STORY: CLAYTON CHRISTOPHER

Growing up, Clayton Christopher was surrounded by

entrepreneurs. He always knew that one day he'd start his own business, but he also knew he needed experience, so he went to work with his family in the medical supply business in Texas. He did everything from sweeping floors, to running errands, to growing a new sales territory from $0 to $800,000 in two years. Though he was successful and armed with knowledge after his time in the family business, he knew that life in sales in the medical supply business was not what he wanted. He wanted to travel more and try his hand at something new. For a few years, he made a humble living racing as an amateur cyclist on the U.S. Pro Tour, but he decided there had to be an easier way to make a living. One day, he had a yard sale and sold everything he owned except for his flip-flops, T-shirts, and shorts. He moved onto a sailboat in the Florida Keys and started a boat charter operation.

In Florida, Clayton had an amazing life as a captain, sailing and entertaining people off the southern coast, but he was barely breaking even. During his time off, he often went on road trips through Alabama and Mississippi. On these trips, every mom-and-pop restaurant he visited served an incredible homemade iced tea that tasted almost as good as the tea his grandmother Mimi used to make for him. He loved the tea but was never able to find anything like it bottled in stores. Around this time, Clayton heard about a guy named Ronnie Carlton from Mississippi, who was running a company called Milo's

Tea. Ronnie's father, Milo, had crafted a recipe for tea that sold more gallons than milk a day in the area. Clayton met with Ronnie and learned more about the business. With that knowledge and his love of the tea he could only find in mom-and-pop restaurants and his grandmother's kitchen, Clayton moved back to Texas to start his own business.

When Clayton returned to Texas, he gathered up $10,000 and his grandmother's recipe for homemade sweet iced tea and started working on figuring out how to bottle and sell it. He spent hours in the kitchen refining the recipe. Once he had a recipe that tasted just like his grandmother's, his next task was to turn a gallon of tea into one hundred gallons. On a tight budget, he bootstrapped the brewing, bottling, and distribution of the tea. He brewed the tea in crawfish pots one batch at a time, filtered it with pillowcases and pantyhose, and used two garden hoses from Home Depot to fill the bottles. Using a Black & Decker drill, he capped each bottle. With the help of a childhood friend named David Smith, he began to make deliveries out of an old van he'd bought with three hundred thousand miles on it.

With no experience in the packaged goods space, Clayton quickly discovered the challenges that came with selling bottled tea to stores. For instance, he didn't realize there were companies that served as brokers that made connections with retailers and distributors to get products into stores. Nor had he ever heard of slotting fees, where he had to pay stores to get premium shelf space, or that stores required money from him to run in-store promotions. Despite a number of setbacks and flat-out nos, Clayton soldiered on, and he and his partner went to every local market and convenience store they could find and begged them to put their tea in their stores. Armed with the conviction that he had an amazing product that tasted better than anything else on the market, he pitched everyone he could the story of a tea made from real leaves and organic cane sugar that was painstakingly made by hand just the way his grandmother Mimi used to do.

He finally found a few stores to stock his tea, and Sweet Leaf Tea was officially launched. However, now he had another problem.

With no marketing or advertising budget, Clayton had to creatively leverage the assets he did have to get people to try and buy his product. He had a great story that people would respond to, and he'd had enough foresight to use that story at every opportunity and even eventually put that story on every bottle. Anytime someone picked up the tea, they would read about his grandmother and the crawfish pots, pillowcases, and garden hoses. He'd also known that having all-natural ingredients would give him a competitive advantage over the others on the market, and it tasted amazing. Every chance he could, Clayton and his team would do in-store demos of the product or give it away at events and festivals because he knew that once people tasted the tea, they'd be hooked.

Slowly, Sweet Leaf Tea began to grow, but there was one retail outlet they hadn't yet broken into—Whole Foods. Though Sweet Leaf Tea was based in Austin, where Whole Foods was based, Clayton was unable to get their buyer to return his phone calls. After a few years of calling the store, Clayton and his business partner finally received a message in the mail that said, "We are not interested in your product at this time." Clayton and David rejoiced at receiving the letter because it finally meant that Whole Foods knew who they were. The letter made them even more determined, and they kept calling, despite the fact that the buyer never answered their calls. They even reached out to the distribution center to see if they could contact a person in that department. It took four months and a lot of persistence, but they finally got into Whole Foods.

Getting Sweet Leaf Tea into Whole Foods turned out to be one of the most important things that happened to the company. Within six months, they became the number one tea in the Whole Foods Southwest Division, and eventually they went on to become a national brand that can be found in all fifty states, in more than ten thousand retail stores. When Sweet Leaf Tea was bought by Nestlé, it was one of the fastest-growing beverage companies in the United States, with sales over $80 million.

Clayton's path was filled with setbacks, challenges, and mistakes, but those experiences helped him get through the tough times and taught him how to leverage each one to grow the company and inch his way to success. Not to mention, those experiences made for future story material.

THE STORY'S GOAL AT WORK

Over the years, I've filmed Clayton at least ten times, either for videos for his companies, Sweet Leaf Tea and Deep Eddy Vodka, or for projects featuring successful start-up founders. I've also seen him speak at close to forty events in Austin. Every time Clayton talks about his company and his products, he shares the story of how Sweet Leaf Tea was created and what makes it unique. On every bottle and in every encounter, Clayton ensures that you know the story of his grandma's tea recipe and how it was bootstrapped together using pillowcases, garden hoses, and crawfish pots.

Through his experience, Clayton learned that he could leverage his story in a variety of ways, depending on the audience he was targeting and what he wanted. When it came to consumers, it didn't work to just come out and say, "Buy this tea." Instead, Clayton learned how to, in his own words, "create a love affair with consumers." The story of how he created this amazing tea using his grandmother Mimi's recipe was a powerful narrative that people loved. Armed with that story, he went to every mom-and-pop grocery store he could find. Soon, every buyer was selling Sweet Leaf Tea, and consumers were telling their friends to buy it. Clayton had used the tale of his grandmother's recipe like a piece of cheese in a trap. He'd used it to convince people that the tea tasted as great as his grandmother's tea, and they bought it.

When he talked to investors, he focused on how there were plenty of brands that had bottled tea in every state, but that there was a tremendous untapped opportunity for bottled tea that tasted homemade, and Sweet Leaf Tea was in a prime position to fill it. He wove in how the brand's "homemade" recipe was crafted by two guys DIYing it. This helped distinguish Sweet Leaf Tea from all the corporate brands on the market, and it allowed retailers to charge a premium for Sweet Leaf Tea. Having that premium positioning and pricing made for more profit opportunity, and investors like this kind of recipe.

When talking to the press, Clayton knew that journalists were looking for a story that their readers would enjoy, and so he hand-fed them the backstory of how the tea was made in crawfish pots according to his grandma's recipe. That tale gave writers the exact kind of materials they needed to make Clayton's Sweet Leaf journey relatable and entertaining for their audiences. Plus, it was a great American business story.

Clayton also recognized that part of his job as a founder was to create a tale to tell by putting it in the hands of his fans, suppliers, and partners. The story of Clayton and David on the bottle making their own tea only added to the image of the fun brand that did Astroturf in-store displays, showed up at music events and festivals, and slung tea while giving away branded T-shirts, bandanas, koozies, and Frisbees.

That atmosphere and image not only helped sell the brand to consumers, but it also worked well for recruiting employees. Different audiences often facilitate different story goals so you can get what you need—in this case, employees. People wanted to be part of this cool, hip brand, and they liked the idea of having to creatively figure out how to appeal to a consumer that also likes to have fun.

What I love about Clayton is how he was able to modify his core founding story and story goals based on the business needs at the time, as well as what he was seeking from each audience. Clayton shows you how the power and adaptability of story helps to meet the needs of the business.

CHAPTER FOUR

THE STORY TYPES

AS I WAS DEVELOPING THE SOFE FRAMEWORK TO help create stories for clients as well as coach entrepreneurs to create their own, I noticed that certain types of entrepreneurial stories appeared repeatedly and wondered if there was a pattern. I looked at a list of the thousands of founders I was analyzing and narrowed it down to the top two hundred. Then I tested my pattern hypothesis on this crème de la crème of entrepreneurial storytellers.

As an ex-engineer, I'm addicted to putting things into spreadsheets so I can sort, slice and dice, and analyze to my heart's desire. When it comes to the storytelling craft, I have been collecting a plethora of information on the entrepreneurs I study, in rows and columns in Excel. One area I started to use spreadsheets for in this regard was to categorize all their stories into groups to look for patterns.

In viewing this categorization, I noticed that there were certain terms and phrases that continually showed up in my interviews. Often, entrepreneurs would talk about how they began their company or a specific moment that led to an epiphany. Some would talk about a catastrophic failure or bad experience that happened. Others would discuss how a deeper meaning led to the creation of their company. What I discovered was that almost all of their stories fell into six types of founding stories: the origin story, the aha moment, the bad experience, the finding why, the problem solution, and the big idea.

These six types represent common experiences that happen within any business. These stories work at every stage of the company and in every industry imaginable. They are proven, universal, and familiar. Audiences know what to expect when they hear these story types, and these types are always compelling if done correctly. Combined with the SoFE framework, they can be used as a powerful reference to create your story.

THE ORIGIN STORY

The origin story is simply the course of events that led to the creation of your idea, offering, or company. Often, it is called the creation story, or simply backstory, because the name implies exactly what it is—how your idea, company, or product came to be. This is the type of story that can be used for the entire life of your company and beyond. Everybody wants to know the origin or founding story. They want to know how you came up with the idea to start the company and the steps you took to get there. Even if you don't use this as your primary story, you should have a good origin story in your entrepreneurial toolbox because you will always be asked about how you started your company.

Drew Houston's story is a great example of an origin story of a start-up that went on to become a huge success. Drew had recently graduated from college and was living in Boston, working feverishly on his software company start-up to prepare students for online entrance exams. He had wanted to go to New York for the weekend to visit friends and figured he could justify the trip by working on the four-hour bus ride each way.

As he sat down on the bus from Boston to New York, he opened his backpack and realized he'd left behind his USB drive that contained all the files he needed. After five minutes of total frustration, he decided he was going to figure out a way he could access his files remotely, 24/7, regardless of where he was. That impetus led him to start writing the original code to what is now Dropbox, an online solution that allows anyone to access their files anytime, so long as they're connected to the internet.

Drew's story is simple and to the point. He got on a bus, didn't have his files, and came up with a solution. It doesn't require extensive detail, just a simple retelling of what happened that led to the genesis of his company. Today, Dropbox has five hundred million registered users across 180 countries and generates more than $1 billion in annual sales.

THE AHA MOMENT STORY

A second very common type of story people love is the aha moment. This narrative focuses on a revelation that occurred at some point in your life. The aha moment is a profound insight, breakthrough, or epiphany that led to the idea, product, or service that your company is working on. A great aspect of the aha moment story is that people love these eureka-type moments. They inevitably want to know what happened next, thus drawing people into the story that much more.

Jen Groover, the founder of the Butler Bag, is a mother of twins. When the kids were young, she was constantly dumping out her handbag trying to find a credit card, her keys, or lip gloss. One day, she was at the grocery store and couldn't find her keys in her bag. As she often had to do, she dumped the entire contents on the conveyor belt to search for them while holding the twins. The long line of people behind her was upset at her for holding them up, but she had no other choice but to empty her bag. As she was leaving, she thought, *There has to be a better way to organize my purse and keep track of my keys.* She kept thinking about that experience and that idea for months. Then one day, she was in her kitchen unloading the dishwasher when she noticed the silverware neatly organized in the utensil basket.

She immediately had an idea. She pulled out the utensil basket, emptied her purse, and put the basket inside. Then she put all the contents of her bag back in the basket and organized everything. In that aha moment, the prototype of what would become the Butler Bag was born. Jen began carrying her "new design" everywhere she went, telling the story hundreds of times to whomever she met as she embarked on the patent-filing and manufacturing process. Jen's ability to share her aha moment story over and over made audiences fall in love with her and her product. She went on to make more than $1 million in her first year of operations and $10 million in her second year.

THE BAD EXPERIENCE STORY

The bad experience story generally focuses on a big failure, personal or business disaster, or highly embarrassing moment that you or someone you know has experienced. Sharing this type of story is not always a natural thing to do, because it typically requires you to describe something most people are uncomfortable disclosing. But herein lies its power. Being vulnerable and letting an audience in on details that are often embarrassing enables you to connect with the audience on a deeper level than other types of stories.

Years ago, Carley Roney, her husband, and a couple of their friends were working at an ad agency and were trying to come up with an online business to take advantage of what was then the up-and-coming thing—the internet. While they were sitting at a café in New York, one of the friends turned to Carley and her husband and said, "Hey, you guys just got married. Why don't we do something in the wedding industry?" Carley rolled her eyes and said, "No way."

The process of planning a wedding and her actual wedding day were total disasters for Carley. She had seven weeks to plan it in a city she didn't know well, and she was working with a very limited budget. When the day finally arrived, Carley and her husband married on a rooftop in July without air conditioning on what turned out to be one of the hottest days in New York in ten years. Her entire wedding experience was a terrible nightmare, and she wanted to forget about it. She didn't want to live it over and over, much less start a business around it. But a day or two went by, and she started thinking about what her friends said. She thought, *You know, I did have a nightmare experience. At the same time, I don't want other women to go through what I did. It was so bad, and it was supposed to be the most memorable day of my life.* The next day, she went back to her partners and said, "I want to turn the disastrous tale of my wedding day and planning experience into a story so that I can help future brides avoid the same fate."

Roney's disaster of a wedding led to the creation of what we now know as The Knot, an online resource to help newlyweds plan their wedding. Carley was able to leverage her bad experience into the cornerstone for her brand. Because of her willingness to share what she went through, women trusted her. Audiences recognized and valued that she'd had a bad experience and didn't want others to go through the same thing. Today, The Knot is a $130 million international brand that sells in the United States and China and has two other brands called The Nest and The Bump.

THE FINDING WHY STORY

The finding why story focuses on the "why" of what you are doing versus the "what" of your offering. It is about the driving force pushing you to bring your idea to life. Simon Sinek, a best-selling author and speaker, popularized this concept in his book *Start with Why*. The "why" is often revealed through a life-changing experience and is layered deep within one's self. Sharing the why is about winning the heart of the audience before their mind. The more you focus on how the why makes you feel—the thoughts, the feelings, the frustrations, the joys—the more you will be able to tap into your audience's emotions. When you start with why, you start with the deepest internal part of your story, which you can then relate back to the problem you are trying to solve or the reason why you want to bring this service to market. Not everyone will have that profound moment when they find their calling, but some people do.

Adam Braun wanted to see the world. As a grandchild of Holocaust survivors and a brother to two adopted boys from Mozambique, he grew up with a propensity to explore. In college, he signed up for Semester at Sea and boarded a ship for six months to experience the world, starting out in the North Sea. Thirteen days into his voyage, the ship encountered a rogue sixty-foot wave that shattered the glass where the navigational equipment was held. The engine lost power, and panic ensued. Nine hundred miles from land in the dead of winter, the ship sent out an automatic Mayday over the loudspeakers. People rushed up the stairs, wondering if they'd have to escape into the hypothermic water all around them. Everyone thought they were going to die.

In that moment, Adam was forced to consider what his

legacy would be if he perished. He began to question why he existed in the first place and realized that he wanted to live a life that improved the well-being of others. He decided his job then was to go and figure out his purpose in life. When he returned home from the trip (luckily, they fixed the ship and everyone was safe), he graduated from school and traveled around the world before he took on a full-time job. He traveled to fifty countries seeking "what else" was out there to help him on his "why" journey. Rather than simply taking photos or collecting trinkets, he would visit some of the poorest areas and spend time with the children. He loved asking them questions and came up with one in particular that he enjoyed asking because of the responses he would get. "If you could have anything in the world, what would you want?" he'd ask. The kids would often want things like iPads and TVs, or to learn to dance or do magic, but one day a kid's answer stopped him in his tracks. The kid said, "I want a pencil so I can learn." Adam gave him his pencil and thought about the plight of millions of children around the world who didn't have access to education or schooling. In that moment, Adam discovered his calling. He knew that he wanted to find a way to get kids access to education. From that point on, Adam started carrying pencils with him wherever he traveled to give to children on his journey.

After completing his travels, Adam spent the next two years working as a consultant at a top-tier firm, learning as much as he could so he could one day start an organization that would truly affect global education and empower youth. On his twenty-fifth birthday, he opened a bank account with twenty-five dollars and started a nonprofit called Pencils of Promise. For his birthday party, he asked his guests to donate money to help him start a school. Four hundred people showed up to his party and donated on average twenty-five dollars. He was so inspired by that evening that he kept working on the idea. A year later, he quit his lucrative consulting job to pursue the venture further. To date, Pencils of Promise has opened four hundred schools in Africa, Asia, and South America. Every one hundred hours, they break ground on another school. By following his heart to find his "why," Adam is now able to share that story every time he talks about Pencils of Promise.

THE PROBLEM SOLUTION STORY

The problem solution story is incredibly simple and common. It centers on why most businesses are formed— someone encountered a problem, they came up with a solution, and they created a business to provide that solution. The more painful the problem is, the more desirable the solution will be because it solves a big problem for the customers. The solution can be real or hypothetical. Even if you're just starting your company and you don't have a product yet, you can hypothesize a scenario where a problem exists that people relate to, and you're building the solution to that problem. The better the results of that solution, the more impactful the story.

As a kid, Ben Silbermann was a big collector. He collected butterflies, stamps, and books. In 2008, he quit his job at Google to do what he always wanted to do—make something that others would find valuable. Though he wasn't sure exactly what that was, he spent two years working on various projects and settled on creating an app that encouraged people to buy things on it. The app ended up being a flop, but he did notice one interesting thing: people used the app to email themselves pictures of products to view later.

As Ben and his team thought about what went wrong and what to do next, the idea of viewing products later sparked a memory of his childhood collections. He reviewed other sites and found that there wasn't a simple and compelling way to share the things you cared about online with others. Despite all the social media platforms that had sprung up online, there was not an online solution that allowed collectors to showcase who they were the way that physical collections did.

Ben and his team then decided to create a website where people could post and share their inspirations with the world, and they called it Pinterest. They spent the next year working on more than fifty versions of the site before they came up with just the right design. When they were finished, they sent emails to everyone they knew announcing the site, but it was a slow start. Convinced that his online solution to building a collection was a great idea, Ben personally emailed every single user thanking them for using his site. To help the situation, he even started holding in-person meet-ups and encouraged users to share the site with others who might love it. One by one they built their audience, and soon it took off. Designers loved the never-ending discovery element, and collectors loved that they could create and curate virtual boards of photos. Ben discovered a problem—there was no way for collectors to display their collections online—and he delivered a solution by providing a website that showed collections in a compelling manner. Now collectors could publish their collections online and gather fans who would discover, view, and comment on those collections.

The problem solution that became Pinterest now has more than 250 million active users. Twenty percent of all U.S. women who use the internet are on Pinterest, and almost a quarter of all users use the site at least once per day. Pinterest receives five million daily pins and more than 2.5 billion page views per month.

THE BIG IDEA STORY

The big idea story, unlike the others, typically focuses on the future and a grandiose notion of that future. Big idea stories are designed to paint a picture of what is possible and inspire audiences to believe that anything is possible if they are open to it. Typically, this type of story requires a high degree of oratory skill or an incredible pedigree for people to believe, but anyone with a big idea can use it.

In 1994, Jeff Bezos was working on Wall Street at a hedge fund. He came across a startling statistic that web usage was growing at 2,300 percent per year. He was so mesmerized by this growth in the space that he brought a pitch to his hedge fund partners. He thought they should focus on a specific industry and launch an online business with the most opportunity so they could capitalize on this growth. At the time, nobody had the insight that Jeff Bezos did, and the Wall Street hedge fund guys all passed on the idea.

Unable to convince his employer to invest in an online business, Jeff took a proverbial look in the mirror and wondered which he would regret more when he was eighty: passing on the opportunity to build a company in the Wild West of the internet or leaving his cushy and prestigious job on Wall Street. Jeff decided he would regret not taking the chance on the internet. He quit the fund, jumped in his car with his wife, and literally headed west. Jeff then began researching verticals to find an industry that was ripe for disruption by the explosion of the internet that was sure to come. What he found was that the book industry was the best one to go after. He created a business plan and made his way to Seattle because it would give him ready access to one of the largest book wholesalers in the country. Plus, there was an ample supply of computer programmers living in the area.

Jeff and his wife found a two-bedroom house with a garage in the suburbs and rented it for $890 a month. He convinced family and friends to put up the seed capital for the venture and set up three computers on tables made out of sixty-dollar doors from Home Depot. In the garage, he and his team built their new website. Once the site was working, his motley crew worked nonstop in their garage warehouse, packing books and addressing and shipping them.

In July 1995, he opened the site to the public. That site was Amazon.com, named after the biggest river in the world because Jeff planned to make his store the biggest in the world. After thirty days, they had sold books in all fifty states and forty-five foreign countries. Soon they were making $20,000 per week, growing faster than anyone imagined.

Jeff's big idea was that you could now go online and search

for any book you were interested in, and you would never have to go to a bookstore again. People didn't even know they needed this, but he painted a compelling tapestry of being able to shop online for the perfect book for your tastes. Today, Amazon is the largest online retailer in the world—accounting for 34 percent of all U.S. online sales and generating more than $178 billion annually.

CHAPTER FIVE

———

STANDING OUT

IT'S A NOISY WORLD OUT THERE, AND MORE BUSI-
nesses than ever are competing for the attention span
and mind share of your audience. On any given day, it is
forecasted that forty million people in the United States
alone are involved in some level of entrepreneurial activity. According to the latest Kauffman Index of Startup
Activity by the Ewing Marion Kauffman Foundation,
540,000 or so new companies are started every single
month in the land of the free. This makes it incredibly
challenging for founders to figure out ways to stand out
as a business. With new ideas constantly floating out into
the world, they all start to sound the same.

We all believe in our heart of hearts that our companies
are going to be wildly successful, and we believe that
they're unique—unlike any other on this planet. We
have to believe. Otherwise, why would we sacrifice all

this blood, sweat, and tears to start our own businesses? But believing that our businesses are going to stand out in this mass of content doesn't mean that they will. That's where your story comes into play.

In the mass of content around entrepreneurship, a stand-out story helps companies set themselves apart from all other businesses, products, services, and entrepreneurs out there. Before we dive into how to actually craft your story from scratch, I want to share with you some of the most important things your story needs to do in order for it to be successful.

One of the best places to start in standing out is with you.

MAKE IT PERSONAL

Not a single person out of the seven billion souls on this planet has had your experiences, and that is what makes your story truly unique. When you make your story personal, you capitalize on that fact. Though traditional business thinking will tell you to keep your business separate from your personal life, in the case of your story, it's the opposite. Entrepreneurship is 100 percent personal, and so is your story. When you start a business, you put everything on the line. The company is you. If you don't show up, nothing gets done. You put all of your time and energy and reputation into the venture—it is personal. There is no need to shy away from that.

When stories are personal, they are more relatable because they're no longer generic.

The personal story evokes emotions that bust through business barriers by creating connection. An audience no longer sees the person telling the story as a stranger; they are someone they know. It is far easier to connect with a person than a product, idea, or company.

When an audience has been walked through the personal experience, they feel what was felt, see what was seen, and live what was lived.

This does not mean that "getting personal" with the audience is the time to unload all personal issues, nor does every single gory detail need to be shared. The audience is not a therapist. They only need to know enough details so they understand what you were going through and how those details—the feelings, actions, and thoughts—relate to the what, why, and how of the business.

Jen Groover, the founder of the Butler Bag, brings you into one of her personal moments of frustration when she talks about having to dump the entire contents of her purse onto the conveyor belt at the grocery store to find her keys. Every time Jen shares that experience, she takes the audience on the journey with her—from standing in line at the grocery store with twins in her arms, to pouring out her bag, to everyone staring at her impatiently.

She shares her experience so that the audience understands why she needed a solution and why she spent the next six months trying to come up with an answer. She talks about how she wrote notes in a journal, looked for options everywhere, and then one day discovered the perfect solution. She was emptying the dishwasher, looked at the utensil holder and its complete organization, placed it in her bag, and found her answer. Jen could've said, "I came up with a better idea on how to organize your purse so you could find your keys or access your lip gloss quickly," but instead she shared all the personal details about her life that built up the frustration to put her on a six-month quest to find a solution. Women who carry purses instantly love her story because they can truly relate to her frustrations.

Her distinct experience sets her apart from the rest. I asked Jen how many times she had shared her story in the early stages of her company, and she responded, "Thousands." The product and story resonated so well with audiences that her story eventually landed her on QVC, where they wanted her to share it with millions of people in their homes looking for the same solution, driving sales for both QVC and the Butler Bag brand.

CARVE OUT A NICHE

When I was just getting started as a founder and working on my first investor pitch, there was a concept an advisor shared that struck a chord with me. It has stayed with me ever since. He stated emphatically that you need to identify the target market you are going after and then articulate how and why you are going to dominate that space. I'd heard a similar concept in business school, but it became much more real when I had to ask for money from investors.

Scott McKain, author of *Create Distinction: What to Do When "Great" Isn't Good Enough to Grow Your Business*, put it more succinctly when I met him at, of all things, a conference for authors. He said, "You cannot differentiate what you cannot define." By this he meant that if you can define the playing field, you can differentiate it.

Carving out a niche is identifying the niche of the business in such a way that where its offering fits in the world can be articulated. More importantly, why that offering is unique and how it can be further differentiated from other offerings, competitors, and market forces is also clear. Often, when getting ready to convince a group of people that the service or product is different from everything else, the audience has already made up their minds that it's not different at all. The playing field is set in their heads already. A story that clearly carves out a niche enables the business owner to dictate the playing field and control the narrative that is about to be told.

There's an amazing entrepreneur named Kendra Scott, based out of my home city of Austin, Texas, who used this concept exceptionally well by identifying an unserved area of the market and weaving it into her story and vision for an idea she had for a new jewelry line. She called it the white space.

Kendra had been working in the travel industry for a few years when she became pregnant with her first child and decided she wanted to create a business where she could spend time with her family, yet do something she loved.

While Kendra was pregnant with her first son, she was put on bed rest. She could not leave her bed, except for the essential things. While lying in bed, she began to ponder business ideas and thought about one of her passions— making jewelry for her friends. Her husband had recently been let go from his job, and they were in a tight financial situation. This spurred her resolve to start a business doing something she loved. She decided to create the type of jewelry she'd always had a hard time finding.

She and her friends all had the same problem. They wanted to look nice and put together, but they couldn't afford the big pieces, and they didn't want to waste their money on cheap jewelry that wouldn't last. At the time, the market was full of overpriced pieces and inexpensive, cheaply made jewelry that fell apart after one wear, but there was nothing in the middle. So she had an idea. Wouldn't it be great if there was jewelry that looked good, yet was still affordable?

She took $500 out of her savings account, which was the last bit of money she had, and started making her own jewelry. As soon as her baby was old enough, she went door to door to boutiques in the local area and told her story. She had identified a space that no one was catering to—women who wanted to look good but didn't have an exorbitant amount of money to spend or simply didn't want to spend. She understood that women would be willing to pay $200 for an attractive piece of jewelry they would keep and cherish, yet they wouldn't have to take out a loan to purchase it.

Her story, combined with a gorgeous product that women loved and an innate understanding of what women were seeking, helped her create a successful brand. Kendra Scott now has seventy-five stores; her products are sold by more than a thousand retailers, including Neiman Marcus, Nordstrom, and Bloomingdale's; and her company is valued at more than $1 billion.

One of the core reasons Kendra has done incredibly well

is because she identified this white space, where no one was currently operating, created a product that perfectly addressed the needs of her target market, and made that part of her story. But brands don't always have to operate in the white space to stand out. If they can communicate their product or service in a way that seems new, or tell the story that no one is telling, they will garner attention.

After John Paul DeJoria, the founder of Paul Mitchell hair-care products, had found success, he was approached by his friend Martin Crowley. Crowley frequently traveled to Mexico to acquire products that he would bring back to the States to sell to architects. On one of his trips, Martin picked up a blue agave tequila and had John Paul taste it. John Paul was floored by its smoothness and incredible taste. Martin proposed to John Paul that they go in together and sell this tequila in the States. At the time, tequila in America was known as a low-end alcohol that produced a bad hangover. Everyone had a horrifying story associated with it from college, and no one in the States was drinking high-end tequila.

They decided that rather than trying to market to the Jose Cuervo co-eds of the world, they would craft a story that would focus on an ultra-premium tequila that the people of Mexico with refined palates sipped on. They custom-made beautiful handblown bottles that came in an amazing box. They gave the tequila a sexy, powerful name, Patrón (meaning "the boss"), and instead of trying to sell it like most tequilas were sold, John Paul went to high-profile restaurants and trendy LA bars and asked the bartender if he could have a shot of their best tequila. In those days, the best tequila cost three or four dollars max. He would thank the bartender, take the shot, then ask for an empty glass. The bartender would set an empty shot glass on the bar, and John Paul would bring out the Patrón. The bartender would gasp, "Put that away." But John Paul stayed fast in his sales tactic and said, "Would you mind tasting this?" The bartender would usually hesitate, but once he had a sip, he'd say, "Wow! What is this?"

John Paul would respond, "That's the future of tequila. It's Patrón."

Once the bartenders were sold on Patrón, John Paul proceeded to ask the owners of these bars and restaurants to introduce their celebrity clients and friends to Patrón. He threw exclusive parties inviting high-profile actors and musicians to attend, and he selectively placed his super-premium tequila at top nightclubs and trendy bars in Los Angeles, New York City, Las Vegas, and Miami. Over time, the buzz spread, and that special bottle was appearing in celebrity photos and being referenced in popular songs. It became a status drink.

They sold their Patrón tequila with the idea that it was

meant to be drunk like scotch and savored like wine. They completely changed the dynamic of the tequila industry in the United States and created a new market—ultra-premium tequila—that no one in the States was even aware of. Today, they own that market niche and are the best-selling ultra-premium tequila brand, with sales estimated at $1 billion per year.

EMBRACE THE UNDERDOG

By the very definition, all entrepreneurs are underdogs. When you start a business, you often have very little in terms of resources, and you are the only person in the business, doing everything. Though almost all new businesses start this way, most people tend to shy away from being the underdog because they don't want to be seen as a no-name player in an established market. They're afraid to take on Pepsi or Microsoft because they worry that they can't compete.

The fabulous thing about American culture is that we love the underdog. We are born in a country founded by underdogs, and we celebrate self-determination, individualism, and perseverance against all odds. When the role of the underdog is embraced, it creates the desire for the audience to root for the entrepreneur. Everyone loves the David versus Goliath story, and they want to get behind the entrepreneurial spirit and watch someone do what no one's done before. They want to see them succeed, and they will follow that person's story to see how they're doing. By embracing the underdog, we can turn our weaknesses into strengths, and turn the strengths of our competitors against them. The underdog position can even change the rules of the game.

What I want you to do is embrace your status as an entrepreneurial underdog. Let your audience know how you are the David to the Goliaths of your industry so that they root for you. In essence, be like Mike—Michael Dubin, that is.

Michael Dubin, the founder of Dollar Shave Club, embraced the underdog quite brilliantly. Michael had worked in media and marketing for a decade at TV networks and magazines while writing comedy and doing improv on the side. He had recently moved to LA to work in online media when, one night at a party, he met a guy by the name of Mark Levine. Mark had access to 250,000 razors and was wondering if Michael, with his digital marketing and promotional video background, could help him sell them. They started talking about the overpriced razor industry and how annoying the process of buying a razor is and what a great opportunity this could be.

Michael believed in the idea of creating a dollar-per-month mail-order membership club for razors and understood the market as a man who shaves regularly. He knew that most guys were frustrated with the razor-buying experience in general. Razors were expensive and had all these features that only an astronaut would ever need. Plus, those blades had huge marketing budgets backed by giant corporations. Rather than positioning themselves in direct competition with the big razors, they decided to go in the exact opposite direction. Michael took the advantages of the market leaders in the space and flipped them on their head. On a bootstrap budget of $4,500, he produced a hilarious video that took potshots at everything the multimillion-dollar conglomerate shavers were doing. For less than $5,000, he communicated Dollar Shave Club's simple business model and used the advantages of the billion-dollar competitors as reasons why people should buy his product and not theirs.

By creating a clever ninety-second video that went on to garner more than fifteen million views, Michael told the story of his company's value propositions by making fun of the dominant players. From that video grew Dollar Shave Club. They didn't need fancy features or big-name stars in ads, just the simple premise that men wanted an easy and inexpensive way to get a good shave every day. Today, there are more than 3.2 million members of Dollar Shave Club, and the company is now owned by Unilever, who purchased it for $1 billion.

Michael's story is the perfect example of a founder completely embracing the underdog role to leverage the attributes of his start-up, while at the same time turning the strengths of the market Goliaths against them. This approach enabled Dollar Shave Club to completely disrupt a $6 billion industry and become the number one online razor company, which was ultimately bought by a Goliath that couldn't beat David.

GET VULNERABLE

No matter how hard one tries or how well one prepares, bad things are going to happen. Mistakes. Blunders. Failures. Catastrophes. Conflicts. Misjudgments. When it comes to sharing bad things, most business owners sweep them under the rug. Either they avoid talking about their mistakes and missteps or they hide them altogether. Brené Brown, *New York Times* best-selling author of *The Power of Vulnerability* and one of the foremost experts on vulnerability, puts it this way:

"To be vulnerable is to risk being wounded, not just emotionally, but being subject to criticism, moral scrutiny or to temptation, as in a point of weakness."

This risk is enough to scare any entrepreneur away from being vulnerable, but what many founders don't realize is that there is tremendous power in vulnerability. Vulneraty is a gateway drug to the heart and one of the fastest and most efficient ways to human connection. People want to hear about failures because we are all flawed. When mistakes and catastrophes are shared, attention is gained. A story that humanizes the entrepreneur's experience helps to build and strengthen relationships with current and prospective customers, employees, partners, and even investors. Vulnerability allows the founder to capitalize on the visceral connection with their audience in such a way that they create empathy from within. When things are hidden or too polished, they become dulled and don't resonate as deeply with others.

I met Brené Brown at the Conscious Capitalism CEO Summit, which I film every year, that gathers together two hundred of the top purpose-driven founders and CEOs in the country. She gave a talk to these founders and executives about how, in order to be effective leaders, they needed to leverage the power of vulnerability. To be vulnerable, you need to go deep and pull the layers back. When you share your business experiences, your audience gets to know who you are. Build trust and connect with your audience on multiple levels by divulging the reasons why you've put your heart and soul into your business. Share what drives you from the inside so that your audience knows your vision is not just a crazy idea but is rooted in determination and the need to solve a real problem or to help others. Share your frustrations and challenges as well, but let them know you are going to overcome them because you know your offering is going to enhance the lives of those your offering serves.

Don't worry what others might think. Your story is your story. People cannot argue how you feel about your experiences that define your story. What's great about vulnerability as it relates to your story is that it makes you more appealing as a founder. Despite the fact that most people think the opposite—that it makes you appear weak and not worthy of leading—it is not true. As Brené Brown so eloquently puts it, "What makes you vulnerable makes you beautiful."

Carley Roney shared all the disastrous moments of her wedding to create The Knot. She put her messy life out there and didn't hold back, because she believed her story could help others. The best stories do more than simply present a believable picture; they captivate the audience and tie their emotions to what is possible. When Life Is Good founder Bert Jacobs takes you back to his childhood and talks about when his father had the car accident that left him unable to work, he creates a powerful connection to the audience with his vulnerability. By opening up about a very personal detail of his childhood—that his family was barely able to make ends meet—he portrays how optimism became a staple of his belief system and internal makeup. This makes the audience care for him.

COUNT ON NUMBERS

There is a myth that you should avoid facts and figures and never use numbers in your story because that is not what audiences care about, but I believe that's hogwash. While I agree that numbers used ad nauseam can bog a story down, they can also enhance a story.

Numbers are to stories what spices are to food. They can be used to provide just the right flavor, accentuate specific elements of the story, and help distinguish the founder and their story. A single number can add a powerful detail to a story that stays in the audience's mind and captures a distinguishing moment or aspect of the story. They can also help to shorten and simplify a story, yet at the same time give the story depth and set it apart from all the rest. Numbers can show the magnitude of the problem being solved, demonstrate the impact of the solution, or illuminate the potential of the business. They can draw attention to a story, add credibility to the storyteller's professional experience, and quantify impressive points of business and life.

I have a variety of numbers that relate to my engineering, business, start-up, and producing experience, but the ones I use are focused on entrepreneurial storytelling. I use statements such as, "I've spent fifteen years filming five hundred top entrepreneurs and have produced eight hundred videos," or, "I've dedicated twenty thousand hours to the art, science, and craft of entrepreneurial storytelling to help entrepreneurs learn how to create and tell their stories."

The many founders you've heard about in this book utilize numbers as part of their story every time they share it:

- Adam Braun traveled to fifty countries to discover his "why," and this led him to the young boy that asked for the pencil.
- Michael Dubin spent $4,500 to produce a ninety-second video that went on to be viewed by millions.
- Bert Jacobs and his brother were down to their last seventy-five dollars and used it to print forty-eight shirts that sold out in forty-five minutes.
- Blake Mycoskie used the premise of the one-for-one business model to bring awareness to TOMS and those they were helping. In the process, he completely changed the giving model.
- Drew Houston embarked on a four-hour bus ride without his flash drive, which led to the creation of Dropbox.
- Kendra Scott used her last $500 in savings to start her jewelry line.

Each of these entrepreneurs uses relevant numbers to enhance their story. They selectively employ the numbers to enrich the story instead of cluttering it.

GO UNCONVENTIONAL

Another effective means to make a story stand out is to make it unconventional. When a story is novel or outside the norm, it is more likely to get the attention of the audience. What's fascinating about this approach is that people actually crave the unexpected. We are consciously or subconsciously seeking things that cause us to pause and take notice, be awed or frightened. Similar to our fight-or-flight instincts, our brains and bodies are always on the lookout for something that will keep us out of harm's way or perhaps give us pleasure.

Scientists at Emory and the Baylor University College of Medicine used functional magnetic resonance imaging to measure changes in human brain activity in response to a sequence of pleasurable stimuli (for the study, they used fruit juice and water) in either predictable or random patterns. They discovered that the brain responded most strongly to the unpredictable sequence of stimuli. The scientists surmised that the brain subconsciously prefers unexpected pleasures over expected ones, even though we may consciously believe we prefer the latter.[5]

Therefore, it can be to your advantage to introduce controversial ideas, startling revelations, or impossible facts.

5   Gregory S. Berns et al., "Predictability Modulates Human Brain Response to Reward,"
    Journal of Neuroscience 21, no. 8 (2001): 2793-98, DOI: https://doi.org/10.1523/
    JNEUROSCI.21-08-02793.2001.

To help your story stand out, it may even be helpful to reveal things that are totally unexpected, astonishing, and private. When you go the unconventional, you step outside the norm and break down your audience's expectations, and they are drawn to what you are sharing.

When Michael Dubin launched the Dollar Shave Club, his intention was more than just to provide a cheaper razor to compete against the higher-priced market leaders Gillette and Schick. As part of his strategy he decided to bypass the middleman and create a mail-order membership model instead of selling through retailers. Key to this strategy was leveraging technology and content to craft and share this story.

The goal was to give the impression to customers that they don't need the fancy razor with space technology. They are much better off with this new product—a good-quality, inexpensive razor, delivered to their doorstep every month.

The idea was to be irreverent and hilariously honest to help Dollar Shave Club not only build buzz for the company but also create a loyal following. All of this became part of their story and positioning strategy that manifested in a video.

Michael Dubin's well-known business-launching Dollar

Shave Club video has several outlandish and bold statements. Lines such as, "Do you like spending twenty dollars a month on brand-name razors? When nineteen go to Roger Federer?" and, "Do you really think your razor needs a vibrating handle, a flashlight, a back scratcher, and ten blades? Your handsome-ass grandfather had one blade and polio," pepper the video. These statements are cleverly done, poking fun at companies that use famous athletes like Federer to endorse their products. They entertain yet have elements of truth in them that make the audience want to join Dollar Shave Club.

The cleverness of the video created buzz and incited people to start talking about the business with their friends. For Michael, it was all about coming up with and telling a good story and building a good sales funnel around customers who were attracted to their story and irreverent brand.

FOUNDER'S STORY: GARY VAYNERCHUK

One of the maestros of making his company, personal brand, and story stand out is Gary Vaynerchuk, founder of Vaynermedia and Wine Library TV. He uses all the elements we've discussed—from getting personal, to leveraging the underdog, to embracing vulnerability and using numbers, to being unconventional—and he does it exceptionally well.

A born hustler, Gary started his first business at six years old and has been developing his storytelling mastery ever since. He started with a lemonade stand, but instead of opening just one, he franchised out eight stands and recruited all his friends to run them by telling them they could make money. Every day, he rode around in his Big Wheel collecting his earnings from his "franchisees." At age twelve, Gary Vaynerchuk had successfully decoded the baseball-card trading business. He made $3,000 in a single weekend hustling at baseball trade shows. Over the next few years, he set his sights on becoming the biggest baseball card seller of all time, but that dream came to a crashing halt at age fourteen, when his father told him to give up his hobby and help with the family liquor store business. He was tasked with working in the basement, stocking and cleaning for two dollars an hour. He worked every waking hour that he was not in school, including weekends, summers, and holidays. But, at sixteen, the whole world changed for him when they let him upstairs to help work the store.

One day, a customer came in asking for Caymus Special Select 1990, *Wine Spectator*'s wine of the year, which everyone wanted, but they were out of it. In fact, a slew of customers kept coming in and leaving when they couldn't get it. Gary was beside himself with frustration, so he decided that for the next person that came in, he would take a back order (even though they didn't have a back-order system). Sure enough, the next customer walked in, asked for Caymus, and Gary replied, "Great. We're sold out, but I can take a back order." The customer gave him his name and address, to which Gary replied, "How much would you like?" The customer replied, "I'll take six cases." Gary, thinking this guy was an alcoholic, asked, "Are you having a party?" The customer replied, "No. I collect wine." Gary had an aha moment. He understood collecting from his early years trading baseball cards. Now he realized that he could turn what people were obsessed with—whether it was baseball cards, wine, or themselves—into a methodology that would eventually help him become one of the foremost experts on wine and social media in the world.

A few years after he started working at the wine store, Gary discovered YouTube. Armed with a mini video recorder and a New York Jets metal bucket, he started Wine Library TV in 2006 as a way to share his knowledge and passion for wine with a community that desperately needed a fresh voice. His show was the exact opposite of everyone else out there talking about wine. He recorded in his basement, wore a Jets football jersey, and used his Jets bucket as a spittoon. He used references, phrases, and examples about wine no one had ever heard before. He threw cuss words around like jelly beans as he talked about everything from wine, to football, to music and clothing styles. His videos were raw, real, and crazy successful. Before long, one hundred thousand people were watching his videos every day. He'd created a cultlike following called Vayniacs, and these viewers became the foundation for his brand.

Through his YouTube channel, he converted thousands of wine novices into regular wine drinkers. He had people like me who didn't drink much wine watching the episodes because they were entertaining and informative. Gary wasn't just fluff, smoke, and mirrors—he knew his wine backward and forward. When I filmed him for an online show called *On the Road with iV*, the host and my best friend, Ingrid Vanderveldt, picked an obscure Australian wine she had received as a gift to see if she could stump him. He not only knew the wine, told her where it came from in Australia, and confirmed what her taste buds told her about the wine, but he also made recommendations as to what food it should be paired with. And he did it all with flair, sincerity, and a confidence that made everyone want to go out and buy a bottle of that wine, because it wasn't about having a snooty, highly rated wine bottle—it was about having something really good to drink with your meal, much the same way you might get some bean dip to go with your chips.

One of the claims Gary made on his YouTube show, which brought an enormous amount of attention, was that one day he was going to buy the NFL's New York Jets. "My next step in my career is going out and buying businesses, then running them through the VaynerMedia machine, then flipping them and making hundreds and hundreds of millions of dollars, and hopefully billions. Then I'll buy the New York Jets," he said.

That was a pretty crazy statement coming from someone sitting in a basement, spitting in a silver bucket, and talking about dirt-tasting vintages, but it was one that got the attention of his audience and stood out like a beacon. He said it with such obsession, conviction, and grandeur that it became part of who he is and what he stands for. He understands implicitly that we all make split-second decisions on what we are going to consume and, in turn, speaks to his audience in ways that they connect with and will be more likely to listen to his words and take action on his recommendations.

Gary even went to extraordinary lengths to provide exceptional customer service because he knew it would not only help create customers for life, but he'd have legendary stories to tell of those moments. He once had a customer place an online wine order from Chicago, and so he started following him on Twitter. He noticed that the customer was making a lot of posts about his love for Jay Cutler, quarterback for the Bears at the time.

He had Kristen from his customer support team—their

Thank You Team—search on eBay for an autographed jersey by Jay Cutler and sent it with a note to the customer that said:

"Thank you for your first order with www.WineLibrary.com."

A few weeks later, the customer sent a return note. "Hey. First of all, Kristen, thank you so much. I'm a hedge fund guy in Chicago. I'm very, very busy. I got the jersey. I love it. It's framed in my office. I didn't have time to write you back. Amazing. How did you know? I just want you to know that I've spent hundreds of thousands of dollars with Sam's in Chicago, which is a great store, but they've never done anything for me. When I walk in the store, they don't even know who I am. This gesture means a lot to me. Count yourself as somebody I want to do business with the rest of my life."

There are countless examples I could share that exemplify what makes Gary such an incredible entrepreneurial storyteller. But if you want to experience his personal and unconventional approach firsthand, follow any of his social media channels, and you will hear his bold claims, feel the effects of his use of conflict, and see the numbers he uses as part of the storytelling cocktail that is Gary Vaynerchuk on a regular basis. Gary is a living and breathing storytelling machine. He constantly shares old and new stories to capture the attention of audiences, bring home his points, and distinguish himself from everyone else in his space, whether it's the wine market, social media, or advertising.

Today, Gary has 1.8 million followers on Twitter, 3.5 million Instagram followers, and 2.8 million fans on Facebook. His YouTube channel has 1.5 million subscribers, and he's written four *New York Times* best-selling books, built a three-hundred-person advertising agency from scratch, and continued the growth of his family's $60 million wine business.

CHAPTER SIX

———

THE KEY TO
MEMORABLE STORIES

IN 1885, A GERMAN RESEARCHER BY THE NAME OF
Hermann Ebbinghaus conducted an experiment to determine what people remembered when they were given
information. He discovered that twenty minutes after
you hear something, you will forget 40 percent of what
you heard. After two hours, you will lose over 55 percent,
and after two days you will have forgotten 70 percent of
that initial information. He called this process the forgetting curve.[6]

In the business world, the forgetting curve can be even
worse. There is exponential growth in the amount of data
we are presented, and the rate of change of that infor-

———

6   Jaap M. J. Murre and Joeri Dros, "Replication and Analysis of Ebbinghaus' Forgetting Curve,"
    PLOS One 10, no. 7 (2015), DOI: 10.1371/journal.pone.0120644.

mation keeps increasing. Although our DNA is such that we interpret, understand, and communicate via story, we still need that extra something to make sure the story is remembered. To combat the forgetting curve, stories need to be simple, have an emotional hook, and create intrigue.

SIMPLICITY

People want and need simplicity in their lives now more than ever. We are overloaded daily by massive amounts of information so much so that we tend to ignore or block out the complicated things. When things are kept simple, they are more easily digested by the mind, making them quicker to understand and more likely to be shared and remembered. Simple, everyday language helps you connect with an audience that might not be as aware of your business or concept as you are. When you use everyday language to explain situations or concepts, they are more likely to pay attention and remember.

In their book *It Can Be Smart to Dumb Things Down*, Doug Hattaway and Jenn Henrichsen explain how simplifying your message or "dumbing things down" helps people understand your message. Their research found that "throwing unfamiliar words or complex data at people distracts the brain, as it searches 'working memory' and attempts to process that new information. People literally stop listening—and miss the whole point," thereby having the opposite of your intended affect.

Psychological research (on things such as website preferences, logo choices, and stock market picks) suggests that when things are easy to understand, they are easier to remember. When information is presented to the brain, the simpler it is, the more receptive we will be to it. If it appears complex, we have a tendency to approach it with apprehension, or worse, to ignore it altogether.[7]

As an entrepreneur, you can have the greatest idea or product in the world, but if you can't communicate it so that your audience can understand it, it's useless. A simple story that is free from clutter and avoids wasting time on trivial details that don't matter will resonate with your audience.

A study done by Siegel+Gale, called the Global Brand Simplicity Index Study,[8] found that 61 percent of people are more likely to recommend a brand because it's simple. As an added bonus, 64 percent of people are willing to pay more for that same brand, meaning you can position it as a premium offering if you so choose.

---

7   Nathan Novemsky et al., "Preference Fluency in Choice," *Journal of Marketing Research* XLIV (2007): 347–56.

8   Global Brand Simplicity Index 2017, accessed November 10, 2018, http://simplicityindex.com.

At TOMS, the simple, one-for-one business model, combined with the story of how it came to be, helped Blake Mycoskie get his first customers, first employees, first retailers, and first press articles. In the airport with that woman who loved her TOMS shoes, he saw firsthand how easily his story could be shared.

When Bert Jacobs and his brother came up with that beret-wearing stick figure and three-word phrase "Life is good," they experienced the beauty of its simplicity as soon as they introduced it in Boston. The phrase immediately attracted a more diverse set of customers who made buying decisions faster and bought more of their product on the spot. These customers returned weeks after the sale because they loved the story their shirts represented, and they wanted to buy them for friends and family.

EMOTIONAL HOOK

The more emotional a story is, the more likely an audience is to remember it. Scientists have discovered that when people are touched emotionally, it triggers elements in the long-term memory. One of the founding figures in research psychology, William James, who studied the effects of emotion on the brain in the late 1800s, once said:

"An impression may be so exciting emotionally as almost to leave a scar upon the cerebral tissues."

Said another way, emotions make the audience feel, and we remember what we feel. The way something made us feel is one of the first things that we remember and sometimes the only thing that rings clear in our memory. Memories that have strong emotions to them are typically stronger and last longer. Creating an emotional hook is about injecting emotion into your story so that your audience has that permanent scar and remembers it in a visceral way for years to come.

A study by Duke University found that the brain's emotional center interacts with the areas related to memory. When we experience something emotional, it comes with a special resonance to us because the brain engages different structures than normal memories do.

In the study, they used functional magnetic resonance imaging to monitor the brains of the study's participants when they were shown emotional and neutral pictures. After the scanning session, the researchers tested the memory of the participants to determine what images they remembered from the session. When they reviewed the behavioral data and the brain scans, they discovered that the memories of the emotional images were more strongly encoded in the brain than the neutral ones were.[9]

---

9   Florin Dolcos, Kevin LaBar, and Roberto Cabeza, "Interaction between the Amygdala and the Medial Temporal Lobe Memory System Predicts Better Memory for Emotional Events," *Neuron* 42, no. 5 (2004): 855–63.

When Jen Groover tells the story of holding her twins and not being able to find her keys while standing in that grocery line, you feel her frustration. When Blake Mycoskie recounts his first shoe-giving experience in Argentina, he talks about the woman who had to decide every day which of her kids went to school because she only had one pair of shoes for the two of them. Howard Schultz brings up the romanticism and communal aspects of experiencing the third place in Italy. He tells you about a place where people came together to enjoy an afternoon reading a book or slowly sipping on a fine cup of espresso. For Adam Braun, it was the look on the child's face who asked for a pencil so that he could learn. When he handed the boy a pencil, he tells you, the boy exploded with a big smile. He relates how the possibility he saw in the child's face became a transformative moment for him.

INTRIGUE

When you employ intrigue, your goal is to pique your audience's curiosity and invoke wonder. Think about some of the best stories you've ever heard. What stood out about them? Why did you want to tell others about them? What do you remember most? Often, the thing that stands out most centers on something abnormal, incredible, or simply thought-provoking. Things that are intriguing or novel are powerful in stories because the brain cannot ignore them.

The unusual demands extra attention and leads to a strong recall by the audience. Russell Poldrack, professor of psychology and neurobiology, and director of the Imaging Research Center at the University of Texas at Austin, used imaging to research and understand the brain systems that underlie the human ability to learn new skills, make good decisions, and exert self-control. What he discovered is that the brain is built to respond to novelty.[10]

Novelty is one of the most powerful signals that determines what we pay attention to because it causes select brain systems to become activated, one of which is the dopamine system. Dopamine has traditionally been referred to as the "feel-good" neurotransmitter because it creates euphoria in the brain. What scientists are now discovering is that dopamine acts more like an addictive neurotransmitter and triggers the brain to want more of the same. "When dopamine is released, it is a signal to the brain that it is now time to start learning what is going on."[11] When something is new and novel, we want more. Think about when you get a new email, text message, or voicemail; you are always intrigued and conditioned to

10 Russell Poldrack, "Novelty and Testing: When the Brain Learns and Why It Forgets," *Nieman Reports* (Summer 2010), http://niemanreports.org/articles/novelty-and-testing-when-the-brain-learns-and-why-it-forgets/.

11 Poldrack, "Novelty and Testing."

want to see what it says. That's the dopamine seeking out the new and the novel.

There is a moving TED Talk that Bill Gates did that created intrigue in a special way. To date, that video has been watched 4.5 million times. Most everyone knows that Bill is the founder of Microsoft, but not everyone is aware of his foundation, the Bill and Melinda Gates Foundation. His TED Talk was about the foundation, and one of its missions is to eradicate malaria. That day, before Bill began his speech, he stood on stage with a jar of mosquitoes and released them into the audience. Then, he proceeded to tell everyone that one of the primary transmission sources of malaria in third-world countries is mosquitoes. I'm pretty sure that every single person in the audience stared at their arms for the rest of his talk and wondered if they would be bitten by a mosquito. I'm also certain no one forgot his speech.

Tim Ferriss, author of five best-selling books and host of a self-created podcast that has amassed three hundred million downloads, is an entrepreneur who embodies the concept of intrigue. From his early start-up days to writing best sellers, almost everything he has done has been against the grain. As the author of *The 4-Hour Workweek* and the subsequent *The 4-Hour Body* and *The 4-Hour Chef*, Tim figured out a new way to deconstruct life.

He used a catchy, thought-provoking book title, *The 4-Hour Workweek,* as a way to grab your attention, and then packaged his personal story and approach to compacting the forty-hour workweek into a concept that exemplified his philosophy on life and success—which is doing the opposite. The guiding tenet behind all his work is to question the obvious and best practices and ask, "What if I did the opposite?"

The 4-Hour Workweek isn't necessarily about working only four hours a week; it's more about gaining control of your time so that you can reduce your hours to a volume that you want "as well as looking at life in a non-traditional manner so you can get the most out of everything you do." What makes the book so powerful is that Tim provides a detailed chronological history of his life that includes all the ups and downs with remarkable candor, bringing home his ideas, tactics, and learnings. It's why that first book sold more than two million copies and has been translated into thirty-five-plus languages. It has been a number one *New York Times, Wall Street Journal,* and *Businessweek* best seller, including being on the best seller list for seven consecutive years, from 2007 to 2013.

His second book, *The 4-Hour Body,* is not a diet or fitness book per se. It's a journal where Tim outlines his "obsessive quest, spanning more than a decade, to hack the human body." It's a way to share the tips, tricks, and processes he learned from the top experts in the world on how to make the tiniest changes to produce the biggest results for your body. His third book, *The 4-Hour Chef*, is not a cookbook; it's a book on how to master any skill in the shortest amount of time possible. It's a book on learning disguised as a cookbook.

Tim is always finding unique ways to create intrigue. When Tim launched *The 4-Hour Body*, he posted a blog titled, "From Geek to Freak, How I Gained 34 Pounds of Muscle in 28 Days" to generate buzz. In an interview with Derek Sivers, Tim said, "People went nuts. It was in *Wired* magazine and linked everywhere online, causing this huge s%$t-storm of comments saying both, 'This is amazing, oh my God,' and 'You're a liar, you douche!'"[12]

People's reactions—good and bad—were exactly what Tim was looking for. He had done the transformation two years prior but hadn't blogged about it until he had something to promote. On the surface, that blog had nothing to do with his book, but it drove people to his website, which in turn drove them to buy his book.

The first time I heard Tim speak was in a Yerba Buena Gardens Samovar tea bar in San Francisco. He had created an impromptu meet-up so fans could ask him

12   Derek Sivers, "Derek Sivers Interviews Tim Ferriss," August 2008, https://sivers.
      org/2008-08-tim-ferriss.

anything and talk about his books. One thing Tim
about, and I got to see in action, was that products
speak for themselves. He learned early on that you ......
to figure out unique ways to sell around a product versus
asking people to buy it. Core to this methodology is that
you have to have an interesting story to tell, and Tim was
living that philosophy. There he was in a tea bar, telling
his story to strangers he'd invited via a social media post
to meet somewhere and talk.

FOUNDER'S STORY: SCOTT HARRISON

If you want to experience a memorable entrepreneurial
storyteller, you don't have to look any further than Scott
Harrison. Scott embodies everything it means to create
great, memorable stories. His stories not only contain the
power of simplicity, emotional hooks, and intrigue, but
they also help further his cause.

After a conservative Christian childhood, Scott Harrison
started to rebel. At age eighteen, he grew out his hair,
moved to New York City, joined a band, and started
drinking and smoking weed. But the previous seventeen
years of his life had been quite different. When he was
four years old, a local gas company installed a faulty fur-
nace in his family's house, and his mother was exposed
to carbon monoxide fumes. The exposure to the fumes
caused her to become extremely sick and unable to func-

tion on her own. He spent most of his youth helping his dad take care of her, going to church, and playing by the rules. Luckily, years later, his mother miraculously healed. At the time, he wasn't sure why, but Scott now believes it was because of the faith and hope their family had for her to fully recover.

After high school, Scott made the move to NYC to pursue being a musician and attend college at NYU. His band never quite caught on and, though he graduated with a degree in communications, he wasn't that into school. Rebellion set in, and Scott became a nightclub promoter. He excelled at throwing parties at clubs. He could get the right people to show up at the right bars and have them pay $500 to drink a $20 bottle of vodka so they could impress their friends. Scott was so good at this that beverage brands noticed. Soon, he was getting paid $2,000 per month to drink Bacardi in public or Budweiser at parties because these brands wanted him to be seen drinking their products. For the next ten years, Scott continued to throw lavish bashes in Gotham for the likes of MTV, VH1, Bacardi, and *Elle*. He picked up every vice you could imagine that comes with the nightclub scene, but he was successful at what he did.

However, around his twenty-eighth birthday, a weekend trip to South America changed the course of his life forever. It was New Year's Eve 2004, and he was staying in a rented house with servants and horses, lighting off fireworks in the backyard and partying like crazy—par for the course at this point in his life. Prior to the trip, his father had given him a spiritual book he wanted Scott to read while traveling. Reluctantly, Scott began reading. The book caught him completely by surprise, reminding him of his youth and religious upbringing. It was also a slap in the face because it showed Scott that he had become the most spiritually, emotionally, and morally bankrupt person he knew. This was not who he truly was, and it was the exact opposite of the person he wanted to be.

When Scott returned to New York, he was determined to make a change. He left the nightclub life and started applying to various humanitarian organizations, intending to serve the poor and find himself. But he was denied by all of them. On top of that, Scott was broke. He had blown all the money he made as a promoter. While searching for anyone who would hire him to do good, he discovered Mercy Ships, a humanitarian organization that offered free medical care in the world's poorest nations via a medical ship. They told Scott that if he paid them $500 per month, he could join their organization. He wouldn't be able to volunteer his way out of his life, it seemed—he'd literally have to pay for his sins in cash for that absolution.

It didn't matter. Scott decided he would go into debt to

make this happen because he was committed to changing his life. Joining Mercy Ships was the first real step on that journey. Scott became their photojournalist, taking photos of everything Mercy Ships did.

His new work took Scott directly into the belly of some of the worst human living conditions on Earth. It was a little more "real" than Scott had bargained for. He tried to leave the ship after just one week. He didn't think he would be able to get through the day, much less the year. One of the ship's chief medical officers came up to him and told him nicely to toughen up. He'd signed up for this, and he would have to suck it up and learn to deal with the tough stories. Scott reluctantly stayed on, and it became a blessing in disguise. The ship introduced him to a world and a skill he had never known. He learned firsthand that many communities did not have access to proper healthcare. They were flooded with disease and illness that basic medical services could easily treat or prevent. He had gone from the cushy life of New York City to the harsh realities and decrepit conditions of third world countries but saw the power of healing and the hope the ship brought to the downtrodden. He wanted to chronicle that story—all of it—in words and photos.

Over the next two years, he became the *Mercy* ship's chronicler and photographer and sailed around the coast of Africa, taking more than sixty thousand photos for the organization. Scott's mission on the *Mercy* was to put a face to the world's 1.2 billion people living in poverty by capturing their faces with his camera.

As he continued to document this suffering, he discovered that one of the main reasons that the illnesses occurred was because the communities were drinking contaminated water. Over time, he surmised that the lack of clean water was the biggest obstacle facing the world's poor. That fact awakened something inside him. He now knew he was going to lead a "life of service" for the remainder of his years on this planet, and his mission would be to address this problem. He desperately wanted to make up for the ten years he had wasted on himself and was determined to make sure that no man, woman, or child had to drink water that could make them sick or even potentially kill them.

During one of his trips back to New York, while still working with Mercy Ships, the idea started to come into focus when Scott was sitting in a club and someone bought him a sixteen-dollar margarita. At first, he was offended that they would spend that much money on a drink after all he had seen, but then the promoter's mind kicked in, and he saw an opportunity—if his friends would spend sixteen dollars on a drink, imagine what they would spend if they could see what that money could instead do for a village in Africa!

He went on to work another year with Mercy Ships, and upon his return to New York, Scott decided to do what he knew best—throw a party for his thirty-first birthday at an unopened nightclub that was soon to be one of the city's hottest spots. This time, however, instead of people buying him drinks or bringing him gifts, he asked his friends to give twenty dollars to attend the party and told them that that money would go toward drilling wells in Africa, at a refugee camp in Uganda. By the end of the night, they'd raised $15,000, and 100 percent of it went to build three new wells and fix three broken ones in a refugee camp in northern Uganda, where there were thirty thousand displaced families and almost no clean water.

That night, Charity: Water was born. Scott's thirty-first birthday party was in 2006, and since then, the organization has raised more than $95 million from fifty thousand individuals and helped fund seventeen-thousand-plus projects in twenty-four countries, benefiting more than 2.5 million people.

WHAT TO REMEMBER FROM SCOTT'S APPROACH

Scott's unique ability to combine the despair of the world's water crisis with the hope of positive change has made him and Charity: Water incredibly memorable. He keeps things simple when he talks about the problem he's solving, the solution he's offering, and the vision for what is possible. He creates an emotional hook through compelling stories that entertain and engage audiences for hours on end, moving them to action.

I'll never forget the first time I heard Scott speak at a Charity: Water event in Austin, Texas. I was completely captivated by his story. He took the entire audience through the highs and lows of his personal journey and shared how that journey led to the birth and evolution of his nonprofit. By the end of his speech, we all had a powerful feeling of optimism that each of us could make a difference in the lives of entire villages halfway around the world.

After the event, I met Scott and got the opportunity to film him for a project. I was able to experience firsthand his unique ability to create an emotional hook through compelling stories. Scott consistently leaves a powerful impression by sharing the raw emotions of his experiences—whether that be from his roller-coaster past, the transformation he went through, or the impact his nonprofit has on the lives of the people it serves.

He describes Charity: Water's mission and actions and paints a vision for the future with an ease and elegance you wouldn't associate with someone trying to change the world. He lets people know that dirty water kills more people in a year than all the wars of the world combined and that one in ten people on this planet do not have access to clean drinking water. He explains the massive global problem that Charity: Water addresses, shares their solutions, and makes it incredibly simple to get involved. Even his slogan is easy to comprehend: *Water Changes Everything*.

Scott and his team are constantly creating compelling and thought-provoking story content that brings an awe factor to the impact they are making in villages around the world. This awe factor makes his story and the story of Charity: Water that much more memorable.

CHAPTER SEVEN

OVERCOMING THE "SO WHAT" FACTOR

NO MATTER HOW GOOD A STORY IS, IT MUST STRIKE a chord with the audience to overcome the "so what" factor. When you share your entrepreneurial story, an audience will always filter, both consciously and subconsciously, the things they pay attention to. They'll ask themselves, *Why should I care? How does this affect my world? And what's in it for me?*

Every parent believes their newborn is the cutest, most precious out there, and every entrepreneur believes wholeheartedly that their business is the most important thing happening right now. The reality is, if you put two hundred babies in a row, yours will look much like the others. The same applies to start-ups and new product concepts.

If you read about fifty new companies, they will all start to sound the same. Amy Cosper, the former editor-in-chief of *Entrepreneur* magazine for nine years, shared with me that she'd receive twenty-eight already vetted pitches per day when she was running the magazine, yet only a few were even considered, much less made it to print. Most angel investors and venture capitalists I've talked to receive five hundred to one thousand pitches per year, yet only invest in four to five annually. Media Dynamics published a study that found we are exposed to an average of 360 messages per day, yet we only respond to a fraction of those ads, if any.[13] Every year, as an advisor to SXSW Interactive, I review hundreds of panel submissions and award competition submissions, yet vote for only a handful of applications that truly speak to me based on the criteria the organization wants them judged on.

What this all means is that not only does your story need to stand out when you finally get it in front of your target audience, but you also need to overcome the "so what" factor when measured against all the other stories, pitches, and promotions they are exposed to. Your story needs to have a special element or specific characteristics that actually matter to your target audience and catalyze them to act once they are exposed to your story.

---

13 Media Dynamics Inc., "America's Media Usage Trends & Ad Exposure: 1945–2014," September 22, 2014, https://www.mediadynamicsinc.com/uploads/files/PR092214-Note-only-150-Ads-2mk.pdf.

Think of it this way. When was the last time that you got invited to and attended a graduation ceremony that was not for a family member, close friend, or important relationship? You most likely went to support a family member, friend, or significant other. No one goes to a graduation for entertainment, unless Oprah is the keynote speaker. Most people have no interest in your graduation ceremony, because it's not very interesting and there's nothing in it for them. However, a good story can convince an audience that your graduation is the best ceremony there will ever be. You can make them care so much that they believe Oprah will be there.

By leveraging one or more of the following elements, your story can overcome the "so what" factor.

THE "BEFORE AND AFTER"

One of the most effective ways to overcome the "so what" factor in audiences is to use "before and after" examples within your story. These can come in the form of photos, video, charts, or simply vivid descriptions. "Before and after" examples are a great way to connect with your audience. By illustrating an improvement from where someone or something was to where they are now, audiences will become intrigued.

A great example and easy-to-learn-from reference of

how "before and after" references are used is infomercials. If you've ever sat up late at night or woken early on a weekend and flipped on the television, you've watched an infomercial or two, and probably have bought something in the process. They may be cheesy, but infomercials are still on television today almost seventy years after they began because they are very effective at convincing people to take action.

Most of these infomercials present products that claim to change your life. They're based on weight loss or fitness, promising to change your physique. Or they're some kind of cooking utensil or lawn tool that is going to save you all kinds of time in the kitchen or on yardwork. As these programs talk about the benefits of their products, they'll show compelling "before and after" photos. For example, with a fitness product, they'll present one photo that says, "Here's what I looked like before I started the program," and another photo that says, "Here's what I looked like ten weeks later."

Often, these photos will be accompanied by phrases such as, "I got my life back," or, "I lost twenty pounds." Whether the "before and after" is strictly visual or accompanied by statistics, it portrays how life can change after engaging with the product or business.

Tony Horton helped build a $500 million fitness empire

by turning every customer's "before and after" body transformation into a story he could tell over and over. He even turned his own body into a walking billboard and personalized story for his business.

By the fifth grade, Anthony (Tony) Sawyer Horton had moved seven times. He was constantly being bullied due to his new-kid status, speech impediment, and nonathletic build. As a teenager, he took up sports to help with his low self-esteem, but at only ninety-eight pounds, he was constantly yelled at by the coach in practice and rode the bench in most games. In college, Tony studied theater, hoping it would improve his speech. During this time, he was told that if he were in good shape, he could land roles in Hollywood. Tony enrolled in a weight lifting class and was lucky to have a teacher who made the class fun and entertaining. He soon discovered a deep passion for fitness and loved the tangible results that came with discipline and a focused work ethic in the gym. Just a few credits short of a college degree and with only $400 to his name, Tony headed to Hollywood to pursue his acting dream. When he got there, he slept on the floor of a friend's apartment, living on Cheerios and yogurt for days at a time. He worked as a handyman, gardener, go-go dancer, stand-up comedian, waiter, and a mime so he could pay the bills.

All the while, Tony continued to dive deeper into fitness.

He joined the same gym as Arnold Schwarzenegger and intensely studied bodybuilders and the techniques of others at the gym. He looked for ways to avoid the bulky, nonflexible bodybuilder physique and focused on routines that would lead to a more lean and balanced body that was optimal for speed and flexibility. He became so good at crafting his own physique that people took notice and asked Tony if he would train them as well. Still pursuing his acting dream, Tony auditioned for a part in Hollywood and met Carl Daikeler, a veteran infomercial producer. Carl hired Tony to be his personal trainer, and Tony totally blew Carl away after only three months of working with him. Carl saw changes in his body that he never thought possible and concluded that Tony had created a revolutionary training program that he could sell to others. Over the next few years, Carl helped Tony turn his in-person training into a ninety-day, on-camera training program DVD and infomercial. That program was called the P90X workout and relied heavily on the "before and after" photos and stories to sell the products.

Today, P90X is the best-selling fitness program in America and has generated more than $700 million in revenue, selling more than four million copies since its introduction. Tony has since written two books, appeared in almost every fitness media outlet, and become one of the most recognizable fitness icons in the world, due in large part to his ability to present demonstrable "before and after" transformation stories.

THE CONSEQUENCES OF ACTION OR INACTION

Another effective method to overcome the "so what" factor is to introduce consequences. When the audience feels that the consequences of their actions will lead to a positive outcome, or the consequences of their inactions will lead to a negative outcome, they will make the choice to pay attention.

Consequences help magnify the importance of the action or inaction because audiences often don't know what they are missing or what they need to avoid. Sharing consequences takes advantage of a human's natural desire to avoid missing out on something or to prevent something from happening. This can be as simple as preying on the ever-popular vulnerability in people called FOMO (fear of missing out), or it can be as deep as saying, "By taking action, this could literally save your life."

The consequences of action or inaction address the "so what" factor head-on because there is a cost or benefit that is uncovered in the story that has meaning to the audience. When Carley Roney talks about the reason she started The Knot, she talks about how she had a terrible wedding experience because she didn't have a good way to plan for her wedding or access to the resources she needed to make sure the day was amazing. By sharing her personal experience, she communicates, "Use The Knot so your wedding doesn't end up like my wedding did." When Blake Mycoskie talks about TOMS shoes, he communicates, "If you buy a pair of my shoes, a mother in Argentina will no longer have to decide which child can go to school."

With Tony Horton and P90X, their promotions and commercials focus on action immediately. You can be fitter, go throughout your day with more ease, have more energy, and feel better in just ninety days—all you need to do is start now. He may reference the fact that your current sedentary state makes you more prone to illness and injury. If you don't act now, your current discomfort could easily turn into chronic pain. By acting now and taking his program, you can transform yourself and start on the road to a healthier and fitter body that'll lead to a happier and longer life.

CREATING A SENSE OF URGENCY

Similar to an infomercial's call to action, saying, "Act now—limited time offer," creates a sense of urgency within the audience. If the audience feels as if they have the inside track on a deal, or information that can change others' lives, they'll share it with their friends and family.

These people can then become powerful messengers for the story and reach audiences that never could've been reached.

The timeliness doesn't have to be communicated specifically in terms like, "This offer ends in twenty-four hours." It could also be more general. Lines like, "Why wait? This course on entrepreneurial storytelling is going to change your business right now," will work in a more general sense.

If the audience is investors, time-sensitive information could be stated as, "There's an industry change afoot. Soon, other people will be entering the space. There is a window of twelve or so months before other companies start seeing the opportunity here. We can change the market together and be positioned as the market leader."

Ben Silbermann, founder of Pinterest, often spoke to the passion of collectors when describing his vision to the die-hard early adopters. These were people who were looking for the holy grail to showcase their prized collections. By targeting their desire to share things they were deeply proud of, he created a sense of urgency. He knew, like him, they were seeking a way to unveil their hard work that was visually stimulating in an online medium the way physical collections were. To many, this was their livelihood or hard-core hobby, and providing this Pinterest outlet gave them an immediate vehicle they could use to display their passions.

He also knew people were looking for ideas for things that had a sense of urgency. Things like an upcoming wedding, how to redecorate a bedroom in a weekend, the best recipe for spicy chili, or what to take on a camping trip were all things that required responses immediately. Ben's story about the power of Pinterest is that people could now actively search for an answer to a problem more effectively than a standard Google search, using Pinterest's collections of curated visual answers to their inquiry.

In the case of Blake Mycoskie, he makes it known that the simple act of buying a pair of shoes today from TOMS provides a young child a pair of shoes tomorrow. Because of your purchase right now, the next day a child can walk to school or help their family in the field. The TOMS story centers on what you can do right now that will make a dramatic impact on the life of someone around the world tomorrow.

FOUNDER'S STORY: TONY ROBBINS

One of the best entrepreneurs I've ever seen make an audience care about what he's saying and make it relevant to everyone listening is Tony Robbins. He exemplifies all of these factors—"before and after," magnitude of change, consequences of action or inaction, and timeliness of action—more than any other. He is the master of getting over the "so what" factor and is one of the best storytellers on the planet. Tony has an unbelievable ability to communicate his story in such a way that you feel your life can be changed immediately and dramatically by attending one of his seminars, taking one of his courses, or reading his books. I had heard about him, read his books, watched his videos, and even taken some of his online courses, but it wasn't until I saw him speak at a live event and met him in person that I understood his true power.

After consuming so much of his content and reveling in his storytelling ability, I wanted to see what he was like in person, so I decided to attend one of his Unleash the Power Within sessions in Dallas, Texas. One of the things I distinctly remember about the event is that when Tony Robbins spoke, I was so compelled and intrigued that I was running to the bathroom then running back to my seat because I didn't want to miss a minute of his presentation. Watching him deliver story after story for twelve to sixteen hours at a time, without taking a break, blew me away. His ability to relate to his audience so that they feel that whatever he's discussing in that moment is the most important thing ever is astonishing. He makes everything he talks about relevant and personal.

Tony's childhood was extremely rough. By the time he went to middle school, his mother had married three times, and a number of his mother's husbands were alcoholics and abusers of prescription drugs. He was whipped with clothes hangers. He had his head smashed into a wall with a fist. At school, he was a small skinny kid who was beat up all the time. He had no interest in sports but started writing about them. He quickly excelled as a writer, and as luck would have it, one of his articles was picked up by *Time* magazine. This led to a job at a local TV station. His mom, however, didn't want him away from home and made him quit.

At the age of fifteen he experienced a growth spurt where he grew ten inches in one year. The newfound height gave him confidence to apply himself at school, and he became class president. Again, his mom was upset that he was never around the house, so she made him resign. At that point, he ran away from home to live with a friend and worked at his uncle's company as a janitor until his mother had him fired and he had to return to live with her. When he was seventeen, on Christmas Eve, his mom chased him out of the house with a knife, threatening to kill him. He knew she didn't mean it, but he never went back.

After high school, he saw an ad in the paper for a sales position making $500 a week selling music club subscriptions door-to-door. He quickly discovered that he was an excellent salesman. Finally, Lady Luck was starting to shine on him. One of his customers noticed his natural enthusiasm and introduced him to Jim Rohn, who was at the forefront of the self-development and motivational speaking industry. Jim taught Tony about seminars and speaking and how to sell to businesses all over town. Jim was so fond of how fast Tony had caught on that he helped him set up his own office. Soon, he was making $10,000 a month at nineteen years old. He was making money hand over fist, but his friends at the time were jealous and stopped wanting to hang out with him.

Not sure of how to deal with the situation, he started spending beyond his means, trying to buy their love and satisfy his needs. Despite everything he had learned about trying to be happy, he sabotaged himself and his business. He stopped showing up for meetings with his team, and the business literally fell apart. His office was foreclosed on, and soon he was broke, depressed, and hopeless. In three months, he gained thirty-eight pounds and didn't want to see anybody. He was in a downward spiral, locked in his apartment, afraid that someone would show up to collect payment on missed bills.

One day, he decided to go for a run near the beach. He was zoning out to the music and began analyzing why he was overweight, unhappy, and out of money. After much contemplation, he realized that he could use those negative emotions to fuel his desire to change. He returned from that run and vowed to redo everything in his life. He would no longer settle for less, and he wrote down everything in his life that he was committed to—money, health, business, relationships. He decided he wanted to create a life he deserved to have and began changing everything—his friends, the things he did, and the commitments he made to himself. He took all he learned from Jim Rohn and the lessons he was learning on his own path to the life he deserved and packaged them into a life-coaching formula.

He started giving free seminars and coaching sessions until he gathered an audience. As more people began to attend his free activities, he started charging for them and increasing the lengths from hours to days. He would do three-hour sessions for $60 a day and three-day workshops for $300. That session I paid for was $1,000 for four days. There are other premium courses that last a week and cost upwards of $10,000 to $15,000. Today, more than four million people have attended his seminars, and fifty million people have bought his books. His DVDs are available in twenty-four countries.

Tony Robbins is one of the most successful speakers, business owners, and quoted people in the United States, and there's good reason. His powerful messages are thought-provoking personal narratives that anyone can use to help them gain control over their lives and make the changes they desire. Every story he tells is meant to speak to you in such a way that it's going to matter to you. He has the ability to turn every story into your story, into something you want to change, whether that be in business or your personal life. When you leave his events, you want to invite everyone you know to go see him, because you want them to feel how he made you feel on this journey.

Tony Robbins's storytelling ability is one of the most unique I've ever seen and completely shatters the "so what" and "why should I care?" factor because he dives deep into every experience he shares about his personal life. He relates the "before and after" scenarios and the consequences he faced—good and bad—and his vulnerability creates memorable stories that stay with you for years. These stories create an emotional hook for every topic he addresses, while simultaneously illustrating the consequences that can happen to you if you let life overwhelm you. He brings a passion and reverence to every experience he shares so that you want to take action immediately. No matter whether you attend a seminar or buy a book or a DVD, Tony Robbins will relate to you on some level or another.

CHAPTER EIGHT

CREATING YOUR STORY

NOW THAT YOU UNDERSTAND THE FUNDAMENTALS
and the key elements that make an entrepreneurial story
successful, it is time to craft your own. If that seems overwhelming, that's okay. You're not alone. A large number
of people I work with are unsure of what story they should
be telling, get confused as to where to start the process,
or fear that their story is simply not good enough. This
might sound cliché, but it's true: every founder has a story
worth telling. We've all had amazing, tragic, crazy things
happen in our lives, and there are lots of ways to relate
an experience you've had in life to your business. You
are unique, and your unique experiences are what will
create an incredible story. The reason this matters is that
almost every successful entrepreneur I've ever filmed
uses a personal experience for their business story.

Carley Roney could've kept her terrible wedding experience to herself, but she shared it with others, and it became one of the biggest calling cards for her business. Her experience turned The Knot into an incredible brand. Imagine if Howard Schultz had simply taken a photo of the cafés in Italy and come back home to work on selling coffee beans. If he'd never shared his experience of the third place, coffee culture as we know it today might be completely different.

When you make the story about you and something you truly care about, it gives you an opportunity to connect with your audience on a personal level. If you do it right and with the right audience, that personal connection enables you to leverage your story to help you get what you need. The beauty of my system is you can take your meaningful experiences, distill them down to the most powerful and pertinent to your business, and use them as the basis to create your entrepreneurial story.

BUILDING YOUR STORY INVENTORY

Before you can begin crafting your story, you need to build the proper inventory so you have everything in front of you to create a *great* story. I call this inventory your story assets. These assets are like the ingredients for your favorite recipe. If you're putting together a Thanksgiving feast, you can't just buy a turkey and call it a day; you must gather all the vegetables, meats, spices, and libations to make the proper meal. This is what you're going to do when you create a story inventory.

The fundamentals for your "meal" are based around things that reference the experience you want to share. Each experience has a set of events, places, memories, ideas, things, facts, people, or dates. The better the quality of the ingredients or assets, the better the end product will be. Great chefs agree that the right ingredients make an amazing meal.

CHRONO HISTORY

If you are unsure about the experience you want to use as the cornerstone of your story, I recommend building a chronological history for yourself, or what I call the CHRONO history. The simplest way to think about this is to imagine an outline of the biography of your life, while thinking how it relates to your business. If you were going to do a biography on yourself, where would you start?

When I'm developing an entrepreneurial primetime series for a TV network, a founder's profile video for a magazine, or an origin story video for a founder's website, I normally build a CHRONO history as part of the preproduction process.

I start with their birth date and where they were born,

and then I break it down into major components: childhood, growing up, and the education phase of life. Then I'll look at their life once they left school—first job, major changes in their professional life, titles, and other key events that may have impacted their business or personal life. That includes career changes, marriage, their first home, hobbies, the book they remember most, their first child if they have children, their first dog if they don't. Anything that represents a memorable experience in their life that might have an impact on their business goes into the CHRONO history.

You can use a similar process for yourself to help you get started. Look back at your life, from your childhood to your schooling, to marriage and your first job—all the major life events that got you to where you are right now in your professional career are fair game. You don't have to be super detailed, but if it was a major event that had a significant impact on the what, why, or how of your business, it can be part of your inventory, and you should write it down.

For easy reference, you can download a CHRONO history template at this URL http://storytellingforentrepreneurs. com/resources/. The template provides questions and section breakdowns to help you begin to create your own CHRONO history.

(NOTE: No need to get overwhelmed or freaked out—I

don't necessarily do this full process with every entrepreneur or project, but it's a great tool to see the various
points of their life from a bird's-eye view so you can find
the important pieces of the story.)

You might have a lot of things you can add to your inventory here, or you might have just a few. Either way, don't
worry about it. In this step of the inventory-building
process, volume is fine. For this first pass, I don't want
you to worry about what you should or should not put
in. Instead, think about the events and experiences in
your life that have a strong meaning to them. We can
add details later.

When I'm doing this process, one of my favorite things
to do is to put all of the events in chronological order in
a Word document. I'll then migrate this info to a PowerPoint document because I like the way you can slice
and dice and move slides around. I like to see everything,
and this method helps me visually understand where
everything goes. I recommend you do whatever makes
the most sense to you. If it's Post-its, a whiteboard, or a
journal, that's fine. Like beginning cooks, it's good to have
everything prepared before you start the process. You
must gather all the ingredients and utensils before you
can cook that meal. You don't need a lot of ingredients to
make a great meal, but it helps to have a nice spice rack,
some protein and greens, and the right knife and pan so

that not only does it cook perfectly and taste great, but you're also nutritiously satisfied and satiated.

CHOOSE AN EXPERIENCE

Remember that the cornerstone of the entrepreneurial story is an experience. Look over your CHRONO history and choose the one experience that you want to base your story around. To help you choose the cornerstone experience, it helps to think about the type of story you want to share as well. If you want to share an origin story like Drew Houston's story with Dropbox, then find the experience that led to the creation of your business. If you want to share an aha moment story like Jen Groover and the Butler Bag, find that eureka moment along your journey. If the story you want to share is of a bad experience like Carly Roney's wedding and The Knot, find that terrible memory. If you want to share your finding why story like Adam Braun and Pencils of Promise, find the moment in time when you found the reason why you're doing what you're doing. If you want a problem solution story like Ben Silbermann's collector's tale of Pinterest, think back to that point in time when you found a solution to a problem you had. And if your company is based around a big idea like Jeff Bezos's Amazon, then start with that experience.

ORGANIZE YOUR ASSETS

Now that you've generated and collected all this information about yourself, it's time to put it together in a way that makes sense to you and the world. I've been at this point hundreds of times, and I know that it often feels a bit overwhelming when you get here, but this is where the CHRONO process comes into play.

For context, let me explain how this part of the process came to be.

As a video producer, one of my responsibilities when getting ready for filming and interviewing entrepreneurs is to prepare the questions that will be asked of the founder we are shooting. I often prepare as if I'm studying for a final exam and my grade depends on this interview. Hence, I spend countless hours combing through online and offline resources, trying to get as much information on the entrepreneur as possible so I know the who, what, why, where, and how of their backstory and company. This is similar to building a story inventory.

For my process, I start with a background research document, or BR3. I've called it that because it took me three iterations to get it right, and my longtime assistant who helped me formulate the process is named Brett Randell—hence, BR3.

This document tends to be about sixty to ninety pages long (depending on how much data there is available online and offline) and includes a wide range of information sources such as their website, home page, company page, Twitter, Instagram, and Facebook. I'll include blog posts they've done, articles written about them, and interviews they've been featured in. I'll also watch videos of them online and have some of them transcribed and included in the BR3 if they are relevant to the research. If time permits, I'll talk to people who know the founder, such as peers, press members, and coworkers. I'll take notes in all these stages and add it to the BR3. This might sound complicated, but it's not that hard, it's incredibly helpful, and it pays huge dividends.

I then take the plethora of information in the BR3 and use it to assemble the CHRONO timeline and history so I can see how they reached this point in time. I'll also include additional sections that speak to characteristics, business model, and interesting facts. The idea is to gather every and any element that might contribute to their CHRONO history so that I can get a basic understanding of their relevant history as well as how they position themselves now. Then I'm able to select the basic elements of their story that relate to a cornerstone experience that I can use to fill in the three parts and five segments of the SoFE framework.

USING SOFE

This process is what I want you to do for your personal story. Here, you're going to take your CHRONO history and use it to populate the SoFE framework.

With the CHRONO history and the experience you've chosen to base your story around, you can begin to use the SoFE framework to find the basic elements of your story and organize all your assets. The SoFE framework should be your friend here. Using the experience you've chosen, take the assets from the CHRONO history that relate to the experience and start placing each asset into its proper category. By the end of this, all five components should be filled.

THE SETUP

With the setup, you want to figure out the what, why, where, when, and how of that initial spark for doing what you're doing by asking yourself these questions:

- What were you doing before you started your company?
- When did you start the company?
- How did it start?
- Where did it happen?
- Whom was the offering for?
- Why are you doing this in the first place?

These questions can help you put the pieces together that represent the background events that will start to draw people into your story.

THE INCIDENT

Next, look at the incident. The incident is the event, the problem, or the inspiration that had a dramatic impact on you or your idea. Here you can ask yourself these questions:

- What happened that changed something in your life?
- What is the problem that you're trying to solve with your idea?
- What was the inspiration that catalyzed you into action, that put you down this path?

The incident encompasses the unforgettable moments in your life. This life event MUST get the attention of your audience and leave them with a feeling of "what happens next?" because you want them to continue listening to the rest of your story. The more impactful the incident on your life, the better you will set up the rest of your story. Maybe you lost your job. Maybe something happened in your life that caused you to rethink what you were doing. Maybe there was a massive failure or you became incredibly frustrated with a problem you were facing. Maybe you saw an incredible opportunity that no one else had discovered. Whatever that moment is, it needs to have impacted you in a significant way so that your audience relates and understands how impactful it was, whether you state it or not.

THE CHALLENGE

Once you have assets for the setup and the incident, you can move to the middle part of the story. The first component of that middle section is the challenge. The challenge is the obstacle (or obstacles) that you've faced. These can be setbacks, failures, or doubt. Utilizing that same question process we used earlier, answer the following questions:

- What challenges did you face?
- What obstacles did you overcome?
- What setbacks did you endure?
- What did you fail at?
- What are some of the doubts you had to overcome?

The more honest, detailed, and introspective you can be here, the more compelling your story is likely to be. For instance, your setback could be that you started to work on an idea and you ran out of money. You had to sell your car, your furniture, and your house and move back in with your parents. Or you pitched your idea thirty to forty times and got told no over and over again. Think about what you were truly scared of. What is something that you are worried that people are going to know about you? What do you worry about that will make people think less of you if you were to share it? Go to that scary place where you have to be vulnerable. These things make for good story fodder. The deeper you go and the more uncomfortable you are about writing this down on paper, the better. At this stage, no one's going to see what you've written. Put it all out there, then you can whittle it down.

THE CHANGE

Once you feel you've written out all the obstacles and setbacks, you can move to the second part of the middle, which is the change. The change refers to the solution or the epiphany. The change is something substantial that happened after all the challenges you faced. It can be an aha moment that brings the story to a momentous, grandiose part, or it can be a decision that was made by you or even for you. It can be called a climax, but more simply, it is a turning point in your story. It could be the thing that caused a course correction in your life. It could be the revelation you had after you went through all those challenges or obstacles. Ask yourself:

- What is your solution? (Try to keep it to one sentence or two.)
- Why is this an aha moment or epiphany?

- Whom is this going to impact the most?
- How will this idea or concept change everything?
- How is this significantly different than before?

Maybe you'd been working on an idea and couldn't come up with a solution. All of a sudden, you thought, *Holy snikees! This is it. This is going to be the next greatest thing since the iPhone.*

THE OUTCOME

After you're done with the middle section, it's time to bring it all together in the end. Here is where we look at the outcome. The outcome is the component of the story that brings the audience home once the change has occurred and leaves them with that target desired feeling you want them to have. For example, the change that just occurred is that you closed your first deal after months of trying, and the outcome from that event is that your life was transformed. Or maybe, after someone tried your product for the first time, they shared with you that they no longer needed to take medicine for what ailed them. Your product had them feeling good for the first time in years. Hearing this confirmed that you were on the right path and led you to quit your job and pursue your product full time.

Here you can ask yourself these questions:

- Once the change occurred, what happened to you?
- What were the results of that solution that you came up with?
- Or, after you made that major decision, what happened?

Keep in mind that the outcome is about triggering a reaction in your audience. You want to leave them with that desired feeling that moves them to make a decision in your favor. When people hear inspiring moments of someone coming up with an outcome that triggers an emotion, they'll think, *Wow, that's amazing. How do I get involved?* or, *I want to support this,* or, *I need to share this with other people.* The key is to focus on an outcome that creates a desired feeling that will leave your audience compelled to take action.

CREATE A SHED FOR THE REST

Now that you've created and organized an inventory of experiences, dates, details, and other information following the SoFE model, you might find that there's more information you'd like to add that doesn't quite fit into any of the components of the SoFE structure.

For these assets, I want you to create a storage shed of sorts to store the extras. These extras are the things that you think are important but are on the fringe of being a part of your story. Rather than not writing them down, put them in this extra place where you can reference them later if need be. They can be funny anecdotes, crazy ideas, or memorable moments, dates, or places. Some of these things might be market data or trends, or other items that relate to your story but you are not sure if they should be part of your story.

In this phase, I want you to be hesitant about throwing things away. If you think it can ever add value to your story or be used in some way, keep it. I want you to keep gathering the ingredients to make that unbelievable meal, and if you start editing yourself now, you might throw away that special spice that could make all the difference in the final taste.

The storage shed is important because it allows you to adapt your story more easily. The more assets you have, the easier it will be to adjust the story to fit the audience. The shed allows you to have a database full of extra material that you can tap into, based on the audience you're addressing. An investor will connect to different points than a customer, and a customer will connect to different points than a potential employee. If you need to enhance or go deeper with your story, the shed gives you a place to grab different anecdotes and threads that you can weave in and out, based on who your audience is and the time you have with them.

Inevitably, you will have the opportunity to share your story with a variety of audiences. This may happen in a thirty-second elevator pitch, a two-minute phone call with a customer, or a thirty-minute meeting with an investor. The length of your narrative needs to be able to change to fit these different situations. The less time you have, the fewer assets you will need, but the more time you have, the more assets you will need.

Crafting your story can sometimes be challenging, but this is a stage of the process that you should enjoy. It's an opportunity to think about everything you have experienced from a third-party perspective, good and bad, and leverage it in your favor to craft a compelling story. Creating your story is one of the most important things you will ever do for your business because it will stay with you forever and you will use it thousands of times. Invest the time now in this exercise to make your story great. This does not mean you have to get it perfect the first time. Instead, revel in the process and look for the elements that are compelling and that you are excited to share. In that discovery process and desire to share these gems is where great stories are made.

CHAPTER NINE

PREPARING AND ORGANIZING THE ELEMENTS OF YOUR STORY

ALTHOUGH YOU NOW HAVE A GREAT INVENTORY IN front of you, you won't need to use everything. Here, we're going to begin to whittle down your assets. This is the prep time for that amazing meal we're making. You could use everything in your kitchen, but that's not going to lead to an amazing dinner. To prepare, you're going to chop the veggies, thaw the meat, premake the sauce, and get out the spices and the correct utensils. You want the right ingredients and the right tools to make the best story possible.

In this preparation phase, you're going to select and prioritize the items so that you're only using the best of the best. You will still have a shed, so don't feel like you're going to have to throw away valuable information. Instead, think of it as weeding out the bad so that the good can grow. When you created the inventory of assets, everything was on the table that was an experience you had, or information to give that experience context and help bring it to life. Now you need to be more discerning. You need to be your own critic. As you move through the assets, you need to be as objective as possible.

The biggest misconception entrepreneurs have is that they think that everything matters, and quite the opposite is true. You want to focus on the most relevant experiences so that you can keep your story on point. Everything in your whittled-down inventory must relate to the cornerstone experience you want to share about your business in some way.

Let's say you were raised on a farm in Nebraska, and you're developing a food product. Those two things are fairly relevant. You'd want to share how being raised on a farm led to an idea for Midwestern meat pies. However, if you're developing a mobile app that relates to monitoring the maintenance records of your car, the fact that you grew up on a farm will be less relevant.

GETTING YOUR INVENTORY READY

I love fresh cherries and obsess over having only the best

ones when they are in season. Every year when grocery stores start selling cherries, I handpick every single one that goes into my bag to make sure it has the right firmness and color because I want every single cherry to taste great. I rarely, if ever, grab a bag of cherries that the store has bagged, because inevitably there will be under- or overripe cherries in their lot, and I don't want to get home and experience a bad-tasting cherry. Getting your inventory ready is similar to this.

At this point, you want to start cherry-picking the best assets from your inventory. Here is where you review all of the assets you have been collecting and separate the wheat from the chaff—the high-quality from the low-quality elements (or highly relevant versus not as relevant). Cherry-picking for your story is analogous to packing for an important trip. You can't take your entire wardrobe. You can only take your best clothes and accessories needed on that trip. The same is true with your story; you only want to pack items of good quality. You may not use every asset for every situation, but you want your bag to be full of the top pieces of inventory that can be used for your story.

This process ensures that only the best assets are used and helps determine what elements are essential for specific scenarios or relegated to the shed for longer-format situations. Let's look at a few elements from Howard Schultz's story.

His inventory would've included these other elements:

- Howard worked in a knitting factory as a teenager for a summer job.
- Howard grew up poor, and his family could not afford health insurance.
- Howard received a football scholarship.
- Howard worked for a consumer appliance company.

These elements, while part of his CHRONO history, aren't all relevant to the Starbucks story.

The fact that Howard worked in a knitting factory in a New York steaming yard is a bit of history few people know about him. That element is rarely relevant to the Starbucks story he shares with audiences. It is not necessarily a high-priority asset as it pertains to that story. However, it's an element he does share in his three-hundred-page book because it is part of his history that he wants people to know about him.

Howard's football scholarship may seem disconnected from the coffee-shop beginnings, but if there is a scenario where he wants the audience to know more of his backstory, he may tell people that the scholarship was his ticket out of the projects. This is an element that is possibly relevant but not always so, or it's simply something you do not have time to bring up.

If Howard is making a point about the Starbucks culture and why it's considered one of the best in the world, he may also include the fact that he grew up poor in a family that could not afford health insurance. He'll add details of his father's injury and subsequent inability to work and how that created a lack of money that dramatically impacted the family. He'll share these details because they are the biggest driving force as to why he made sure that Starbucks offered health insurance not only to full-time employees but to part-time employees as well. This is a fairly relevant element, depending on the story being told.

Not everyone knows that Howard Schultz worked for a consumer appliance company before he founded Starbucks. It's a detail he shares depending on the audience he is talking with, the amount of time he has to share his backstory, and what he is trying to accomplish by sharing his story. This is another instance where the element could or could not be relevant to the story or could be omitted if you want to keep your story short.

In a three-hundred-page book, people are curious about his background, so they'll read through his life story, but if he's giving a three-minute pitch, does anyone really care? Probably not. When they hear Howard share his story, they are mainly interested in how he came up with the idea for the Starbucks brand and how he got there.

The core elements of Howard's story are that he traveled to Italy and wanted to create that same experience of the third place back in the United States. You don't necessarily need to know that he worked at an appliance company previously, or about his football scholarship. They're interesting facts, but they don't necessarily make the audience more emotionally connected to the story. In fact, if there are too many extra elements, they might distract the audience from the story Howard wants to tell.

As you go through your inventory, you can improve on it by removing the bad apples—the assets that are not relevant or don't add value to your story. You can go through your inventory and look for the bad apples and say, "Nah, that's a dumb idea," or, "Nobody's going to care about that," or, "The fact that I got a 4.0 in grad school doesn't pertain to my food-service product idea." Often, your gut is a good guide to help you figure out what's really good or really bad. Listen to it. If you keep in mind that less is more, and that the quality of the input equals the quality of the output, it will help guide you through this process.

I want you to look at all the elements in front of you and ask yourself these questions:

- What can be removed?
- What's irrelevant?
- What's uninteresting or too confusing?

At this point, I like to go through the list and put check marks or stars by the assets that are important in each component. Don't overthink anything. Simply look at each asset and determine if it's important, relevant, interesting, or critical to the story. Once you get through all the assets of the inventory, circle back through and do it again. If you still think something's important, then put another star or check by it. Do this until the end of the list. Now, if you still feel there are too many elements left, I want you to do a third pass.

The items that have the most stars beside them are going to be the ones you take with you to the next stage of creating that great meal.

If you're still having trouble whittling down your assets, you might want to bring in a third party. Up to this point, it's been you alone with your story, and an objective outsider can be very helpful. Give them an overall idea of where you're at with your narrative (story), and then go through the list of assets and ask, "Do you think this is interesting, relevant, or compelling?" Look for their first reaction as that will be the most truthful.

FOUNDER'S STORY: SARA BLAKELY

Sara Blakely was in her twenties when she decided to follow in her father's footsteps and go to law school. However, her plans were quickly upended when she failed the law school exam twice. Luckily, thanks to a childhood lesson, that did not dissuade her from moving her life forward. At the dinner table when she was growing up, Sara's father would always ask, "What did you fail at this week?" If there were no failures, her dad would be disappointed. He made failure a positive, and it's been a key ingredient to her formula for success. When she failed the law school exam, she decided to do something fun and moved to Florida to work at Disney World. She immediately got a job as a ticket seller, but her heart was set on playing the character Goofy. She tried out for the part, but it turned out she was too short for the position (she was five foot seven and you have to be five foot eight). They told her she could be a chipmunk instead, but Disney has a rule that you have to wait three months before you can try out for a new position, so she was stuck selling tickets at the park for the time being. This was not the position she wanted, so she quit and started selling fax machines to make a living. While this was not her ideal pursuit, she kept at it because she felt that one day she would come up with a unique product idea and start her own company.

Selling anything door-to-door is hard, but selling fax machines in Florida in the summer was extremely tough. Because of the heat, she wanted to wear open-toed shoes, but the problem was that pantyhose looked terrible with those types of shoes. And she wanted to wear pantyhose so that her butt looked good in her white pants. To fix her problem, Sara cut the feet off her pantyhose so that she could still get the effect of the control-top pantyhose without the visible evidence on her feet. This was the unique product idea Sara had been waiting for. At the time, she couldn't find anything else like it on the market, and she spent the next two years working on designs, a name, and packaging for what this would be.

Once she'd fleshed out her idea into a solid viable product, she wanted to file a patent, but no one would help her. No one would take her idea seriously, and she didn't have enough money to hire a lawyer. Emboldened by the lessons on failure she'd learned as a child from her father, she didn't let these setbacks slow her progress. Sara went to the library, researched how to submit her own patent, and spent two years in the process, all while still selling fax machines.

After the patent was filed, she went to manufacturing companies with the intention of creating a compelling prototype with great packaging. She went up and down the southeast coast, but all of the manufacturing companies told her it was a terrible idea. The problem with every one of these companies was that they were all run by men, and although they were already making women's undergarments, they didn't think her idea would work.

Luckily, one of the men who told her no happened to have

two daughters. That night, after he had rejected Sara and her idea, he went home and told his daughters the idea. They thought their dad was crazy for turning Sara down and convinced him that it was a great idea. The next day, the manufacturer called Sara, told her what had happened when he shared her story with his daughters, and said he was in. Elated, Sara moved on to the next challenge, which was packaging.

Sara looked at the hosiery space and realized that she'd been looking at the same half-naked woman in a photograph on top of a package that was always beige and gray. She knew she wanted her packaging to be bold and different, so she chose the color red and placed three cartoon-illustrated women on the cover to make sure her product uniquely stood out. Once she had the packaging, prototype, and a clever name she'd created herself, she decided to call the Neiman Marcus store in Atlanta and pitch them the product. They told her that she had to call the buying office in Dallas—she didn't know that there was such a thing as a buying office. Sara called Dallas, introduced herself, and talked about her product that was going to change the way women wore clothes. The woman agreed to give Sara a ten-minute meeting if she would fly to Dallas.

Sara bought a ticket to Dallas and boarded the plane with her lucky red backpack, which she'd had since college and had taken with her to every meeting since she started working on the idea. Her friends urged her not to take the bag, even pleaded with her to buy a Prada bag and return it the next day if she had to, but Sara took her red backpack anyway. Sara arrived at the Dallas Neiman Marcus offices ready to pitch her product. With her footless Spanx in tow, a color copy of the packaging she had created on her friend's computer, and her lucky backpack, Sara began her presentation. About five minutes into it, she realized the buyer wasn't completely impressed. That's when Sara got the idea for her own "before and after." Sara took the buyer into the bathroom and showed her what she looked like in her pants with and without the prototype on. The buyer from Neiman Marcus was so impressed that she placed an order for seven stores.

Today, Spanx generates $300 million in revenue, is sold in more than thirty countries, and is estimated to be worth more than $2 billion. Sara is the youngest self-made female billionaire in history, owns 100 percent of her company, and has never spent a dime on advertising.

Sara always tells a compelling story that is memorable and relatable. The core of her story centers on finding a solution to a problem that she dealt with on a daily basis. She wanted her butt to look good in white pants, but she didn't want to wear pantyhose with open-toed shoes, so she cut the feet off her pantyhose. What makes her and her story so endearing and entertaining is all the little things she shares that make it come alive. She weaves in hand-selected elements of her background and experiences that showcase who she is, what matters to her, and why she kept going. All of these things make you root for her along the way and make you wonder what will happen next. And, if you have a similar need, they'll make you want to buy her product.

As you go through your chronological history, you will want to follow Sara's example and find those elements to include that let your audience know who you are, why you do what you do, and how you got to where you are. They don't have to be polished, beautiful, and elegant, but they do have to be interesting, compelling, and something you're proud of or need to share. Your story doesn't have to be amazingly fluid, but you do need a powerful core foundation for your story, peppered with colorful elements. Like Sara's clunky red backpack, cut-off pantyhose, and ragtag way of getting things done, you can leverage your hand-selected items to help tell your story so people root for you, the same way we root for her.

If I were creating Sara's story from scratch, I would've used the same process I've created and shared with you. I would create the BR3 research document, then cherry-pick the elements that stood out the most. I would find the ones that were funny, striking, entertaining, extraordinary, or just interesting and make a list of them in a semi-chronological order like so:

- When she was growing up, her father would ask her what she failed at every week.
- She wanted to go to law school, but she failed the LSAT twice.
- She went to Disney World and did not get the job as Goofy.
- She sold fax machines door-to-door in Florida during the summer.
- She wanted her butt to look good in white pants.
- She cut off the feet of her pantyhose.
- She worked for five years selling fax machines.
- She spent time in the library learning how to file her own patent because she didn't have enough money for a lawyer.
- She traveled up and down the southeast coast to visit manufacturers and was told no by all of them.
- She met one manufacturer who initially said no but changed his mind after he mentioned it to his daughters.
- She took her prototype and her little red backpack and visited stores.
- She flew to Dallas to visit the buyer after the buyer agreed to give her ten minutes.
- She took the buyer into the bathroom to visually

demonstrate how it made her butt look before and after wearing Spanx.

- The buyer agreed on the spot to order for seven stores.

Now that you've seen how I would hand-select elements for Sara's story, look at your own cherry-picked assets and see if they still make sense. Do they stand out? Are they entertaining? Are they interesting and compelling? If not, choose new ones, or shape them in such a way that they are. The fact that Sara got a job at Disney World may be interesting but not necessarily relevant to the story. What makes it relevant is sharing how Sara dealt with failure when she didn't get the job she wanted. Taking elements that aren't necessarily relevant and adding an angle or context to them will help them become more relevant.

CHAPTER TEN

CONSTRUCTING YOUR STORY

NOW THAT YOU'VE DONE ALL THE PREP WORK, IT'S time to start experimenting with putting it together. Before you begin, it helps to do a review of the steps you've taken to get to this point. Those steps are the following:

1. Decide which "story type" you want to use.
2. Select the experience you are going to focus on that will be the basis for your story.
3. Build your story inventory using the CHRONO history.
4. Select the best assets from your inventory to shape your experience into a story.

If you have skipped over any of these steps, I highly recommend that you complete them before proceeding.

They are vital to your story. These steps prepare you for the construction process, and I want you to be ready to craft your story, because starting this process can often be the most daunting part of creating your story. This is where the rubber hits the road and founders find themselves staring at a blank page, waiting for inspiration.

The key to get over this hump is to simply "start" creating your story. You can start at the beginning, but often, it's easiest for founders to begin with the asset they are most comfortable with or the one that feels the most compelling. Just as when you were building your inventory and you weren't sure where to start, you should start at the point that is most interesting to you or that flows for you.

When I started working on the Drew Houston story, the thing that kept resonating with me was his experience of forgetting the flash drive when he embarked on that four-hour bus ride. I've lived and breathed many similar moments—forgetting an external hard drive or forgetting to save a file to my laptop when I was traveling—and I've experienced the frustration of not being able to do the work. For Drew Houston's story, I began at that point when he realizes he forgot his hard drive and worked forward and backward from it. When recounting the story of John Paul DeJoria, the founder of Paul Mitchell and Patrón, I typically start with the fact that he was a guy who had been fired from every job he'd had. He was living in his car with his child when he scraped together his last $700 to start Paul Mitchell hair-care products. I start with this point because it immediately sucks the audience in. Almost anyone I've ever talked to about John Paul wants to hear more after they hear that detail.

I want you to find that moment in your inventory that keeps grabbing your attention, and I want you to start there. If you can't find any shiny objects, dig down and start shining them yourself. There is gold in the feelings, sensations, and mental gymnastics we all go through when starting companies—you just need to let it all out so the world knows what it looks and sounds like. Relive what you felt when the incident happened, describe how your challenges made you feel, and tap into that aha moment that changed everything.

If you're having difficulties here, an objective third party can help you look at the cherry-picked items in your inventory and tell you whether they're interesting or compelling. I often find that when I'm talking to people and they start sharing their story, they'll mumble through some of the most interesting parts because they've told them so many times that they no longer seem interesting. They gloss over an element of their story because they don't think it matters that much to an audience, even though it's the part that people want to hear the most. Don't gloss over any details. An objective friend, mentor, or colleague can help you find the provocative parts of your story.

As you begin to construct your narrative, you're going to go back to the SoFE formula and use it as a framework to put everything together. That framework of beginning, middle, and end is meant to be "plug and play" so that you don't have to overthink anything.

PUTTING SOFE TO WORK

For context, let's use a story I created for my Storytelling for Entrepreneurs online course, CREATE Your Story from Scratch, which centers on a hypothetical product and app called FindMyFourLegger.com. I'm going to walk you through the process I would have used to create the story. The premise of the product is that it helps you find your pet if it is lost. Using a GPS device on its collar, you can track your pet's location using a mobile device. Though I did not actually make the product, it is based on an actual event and experience that happened to me— losing my dog, Fitty G, when he ran off.

SELECT THE STORY TYPE

This is the first step in the process. For the FindMy-FourLegger.com concept, I'm going to use the origin story because I know that every person I tell my concept to who owns a pet is going to ask me how I came up with the idea. It's simple, straightforward, and easy to remember.

CHOOSE THE EXPERIENCE

The idea for the Find My Four Legger app came from the experience of me coming home one night to find my dog was gone. What happened after I discovered this is also part of my experience that directly relates to why I came up with the idea.

DETERMINE THE STORY GOAL

I want audiences to know the unconditional love pet owners have for their pets and the lengths we'll go to in order to make sure they are safe and cared for.

CREATE STORY ASSETS AND CHRONO HISTORY

Using the experience of losing my dog, I list out the sequence of events, thoughts, and feelings that center around my experience of coming home to find Fitty G gone. I also look at my history and include things that might be relevant or compelling to that experience in my CHRONO history. Remember, this is the part that includes the most information, so anything that relates to the experience goes here.

PREP THE INVENTORY

I then cherry-pick the parts from that CHRONO history that I think will resonate with my target audience the most. These are things like how special my dog is to me, how much I love it when my dog greets me, or the pit of despair my heart sank into when I found him gone. I don't select things like Fitty G's age or the type of house or neighborhood I live in, as they're not compelling parts of the experience.

USE THE SOFE FRAMEWORK

Once I have the best parts selected, I put those assets into the three parts and five components of the SoFE framework. I select assets that help tell the sequence of events in the shortest and most compelling way.

Here is how I set up the SoFE framework table for Find-MyFourLegger.com.

BEGINNING	SETUP:
	I love my dog. He is one of the most important things in my life—he is my best friend, child, brother, and confidant.
	Few things on this earth compare to the time I get to spend with him and the greeting I get from him when I come home and he acts as if I am the second coming—regardless of whether I've been gone ten minutes or ten hours.
	INCIDENT:
	One night, after I was out for dinner at a friend's house, I came home and my dog was gone. The dog door was open and the backyard gate had somehow been left open, and I couldn't find him anywhere.
MIDDLE	CHALLENGE:
	Totally freaked out that my dog was gone, I started searching all over the neighborhood.
	I knocked on neighbors' doors, called the dog pound, and even asked my best friend to come over and help me look. I was sick to my stomach thinking that I'd lost my dog and, even worse, that something bad may have happened to him.
	CHANGE:
	Luckily, after two frantic hours of searching and freaking out, I found him at a neighbor's house, having a good time making new friends. But my mind wouldn't stop racing—there had to be a way to prevent this from happening in the future and to help others address this issue as well. I couldn't be the only one who had lost their dog and had no good way to find it. I started trying to think of a way that I could find my dog in the same way I could find my phone. I'm not a programmer, but I knew there had to be a way to put something on the dog—either on its collar or in its chip—so I could get on my computer and find it anytime I wanted. I spent the next four weeks trying to figure out all the moving parts and what it would take to get this going.
END	OUTCOME:
	I created an app called FindMyFourLegger.com for anybody who's ever lost their pet or couldn't find them, so they wouldn't have to go through the gut-wrenching fear I experienced. With this app, they can simply go online to figure out where they are. I've told this story to thirty of my friends who have pets, and twenty-nine of them have already signed up.

Once complete, I trim the framework down to three bullet points so as to help stay focused and keep it simple.

- I love my dog more than anything. One night after going to dinner at a friend's house, I came back to find him missing.
- I searched frantically all over the neighborhood, getting more worried by the minute. I luckily found him hours later.
- Knowing that other owners face this fear, I came up with the idea for an app that works like the Find My iPhone app but for pets.

This is also a great exercise to help you trim down your story from pages to bullets when you feel that it's too long. It facilitates getting to the core essence of the three parts of your story.

WRITE OUT YOUR STORY

Now that you have all your assets organized utilizing the SoFE framework and you've cherry-picked the best of the best, I want you to write your story down. There's no substitute for writing a story down, because it forces you to start putting it into an organized manner that you can easily work with. Seeing it in a written format helps you identify problems and challenges. How you write it down is up to you. It can be in full paragraph form, or it can be bullet points. It could even be in PowerPoint if that works for you. In fact, if you hate writing, say your story out loud while recording it, and then transcribe it so you can review it on screen or paper. Simply pick the medium of choice that enables you to get a version of your story down that you could send to someone else to review. You're not going to send it anywhere just yet, but I want you to have something you can read and review easily.

To start writing, I use the elements of the SoFE framework table and the work I've done in the steps above, and I write out the story as if it were going to go in the "My Story" section of my website. The beginning of the process would look like this:

When I came home one day and found that my dog, a beloved and hip cocker spaniel named Fitty G (named after the rapper 50 Cent), was not in my house or the backyard, I completely freaked out. My four-legged best friend was gone. In an instant, I was devastated and beside myself that the worst had happened to him. I then proceeded to frantically search the neighborhood. Eventually I found him, a few hours later, buddying up to some folks who lived a few blocks over. As I was walking home with Fitty G, I knew millions of other pet owners had probably experienced the same thing I went through, so I came up with an idea to create a GPS tracking device that would live on his collar so that I could pull up my phone and click on an app that would show me where my dog was in real time. This way, no dog or cat or ferret owner would ever have to worry about losing their pet, because they'd always know where it was.

To come up with the story, I started to think about what I would include in the beginning that would grab people's attention. I started asking myself where the idea came from. For me, the idea came from the fact that one night I came home and my dog was gone. He wasn't in the house or the backyard, and I saw that the gate was open. In that moment, I went into a state of sheer panic.

Right there, as I'm sharing this part of the story with you about what happened to me in that moment, I'm giving you the setup and the incident. I went out for an evening last fall, and when I came home that night, my dog was gone. It doesn't take a whole lot more than that. If you've ever owned an animal, you're going to know what that feeling is like immediately. It will hit you right in the gut, and it will resonate. I then tell them that I was in a sheer state of panic. By telling them what physically transpired in real life, I'm able to start sucking them into the story.

I share the challenges I faced. I was scared half to death that something had happened to my dog, so I called the shelters, the vets, everywhere. I built tension by talking about the obstacles and setbacks I was facing in trying to find my dog. Eventually, I found my dog, and I was so relieved, but I couldn't help but think, *Wouldn't it be great if I could've looked at my phone and immediately found where he was?*

In my story, that is the change. It's the epiphany and the lightbulb moment that led to my product, FindMyFour-Legger.com, which is a cool little app that helps anyone find their dog in real time.

In a very short amount of time, I set up what happened. I gave you the incident that my dog was gone. I took you through the challenges that I faced, both physically and emotionally, and I told you the resolution, that, thank goodness, I found him. Then I shared that after finding my dog, I had an epiphany and created my product. The outcome was that I decided to make this product so that no one would ever have to experience what I had in those moments when my dog was missing.

When you walk yourself through this process, you can get as detailed as you want in the inventory and cherry-picking stages. I could have added that I was at a dinner party at a friend's house that night before I came home, but would that add to my story? Probably not. People might not connect with me in a very strong way if I'd said that I'd gone out to a dinner party. However, if I said that I was at a friend's house playing with their dog and I couldn't wait to get home to see my own, then that probably would add to my story. It would let the audience know how important my dog was to me and accentuate the next part of the story, where I discover my dog is missing.

CHAPTER ELEVEN

REVIEWING AND REVISING YOUR STORY

NOW THAT YOU HAVE A DRAFT STORY IN PLACE, it's time to review and revise. The revision phase allows you to see how your story looks, sounds, and feels and lets you revise accordingly if it's not up to snuff. In this phase of the story creation process, I like to apply what I call "reality filters." This DIY technique helps you prepare for the variety of objections, situations, questions, and reactions that you'll receive in the real world.

Whenever you share your story, people will apply these filters to you, both subconsciously and consciously. We use filters as protective systems to help us make decisions daily so that we don't become overwhelmed. Whether you like it or not, this is how the human brain works. Every day, we are being asked to make hundreds of choices about what to consume and not consume. We are bombarded with choices on what meetings to take, what phone calls to answer, what emails we open, what books we read, or what movies we watch—always deciding what to tune out or tune in based on our needs or interests.

In this phase, I want you to become your own critic. The good news is, you are already an amazing critic because you exist in this world. You already use the same reality filters that your audience will use. You are constantly deciding what to pay attention to through your own filters of preferences and tastes. You have no problem giving an opinion on anything that impacts your life, from the car you drive, to the food you eat, to the clothes you wear. Now you can use that same inner-critic process when it comes to evaluating your own story.

There are a number of key challenges that your story will face when you take it out into the real world. These challenges are the same ones that you use daily to evaluate what to tune into. Here are three of the biggest you will face, which you can start to prepare for.

TIME

People are almost always willing to hear a short pitch or look at something that won't take much time. One of the biggest mistakes entrepreneurs make is taking too much time to convey their story. It's not that people don't like long stories. They do. It's more that short stories have a better chance of being heard, because they're indeed short, and they are more likely to be listened to all the way through. And when stories are short (and good), they tend to be shared more often than longer ones, for the simple reason that people can remember them more readily and repeat them more easily.

Founders believe they need to tell you everything about their idea, when in fact, stories that are shorter can be just as powerful and sometimes more compelling because they stir the imagination. There's a famous tale about novelist Ernest Hemingway. He was reportedly once challenged to write a story in under ten words for ten dollars. He did it in six:

"For sale: baby shoes, never worn."

Though this tall tale has proven elusive in terms of whether Hemingway actually wrote it, the point is well made. These six words not only give you a sense of what happened—the story, if you will—but they simultaneously ignite the imagination and catalyze your emotions. You immediately try to determine what it means and how it came to be, and it leaves you wanting more. And that is exactly what you want—your audience wanting more of what you have to share or offer.

Nine times out of ten, when you tell your story for the first time, it's going to be too long. Although you have a lot to say, you are more than likely going to want to shorten it. What most people don't realize is that making things shorter is often more difficult than making things longer. But I've come up with a technique I use to help me, whether I'm trying to figure out what to cut from a video or giving tips to an entrepreneur on what to trim from their story.

One of the best ways to shorten your story is to condense it down to three simple bullet points. Similar to how I did with FindMyFourLegger.com at the end of chapter 10, I want you to boil down each section—beginning, middle, end—to one bullet point, no paragraphs or super-long sentences. Those short and succinct bullet points should be as such:

- In the beginning this happened.
- In the middle this happened.
- In the end this happened.

By doing this, you will start to eliminate extraneous information that is most likely inessential to the core of the story. When you go from pages to bullets, you take out all the excess noise and clutter and boil it down to the primary essentials. These resulting bullet points may not feel like a full story to you, but trust me, they will help you make your story more concise. By focusing on an economic approach to words when it comes to the final story you share, you will have a story people will want to hear.

COMPREHENSION

The second challenge you will face in the real world is comprehension. The people you share your story with need to understand, or their attention will drift and they'll ignore you.

To make your story easier to understand, remove buzzwords, lingo, and jargon that are specific to your industry. Do your best to avoid academic or highly technical terms, even if you, your offering, or your industry is complex. At times, you may find a situation where these are appropriate, but for all intent and purposes, it's better to remove these things. An audience doesn't want to waste time figuring out what your product does or what your business offers, so don't tax the brains of your audience by forcing them to figure out complicated offerings. If you overload their limited store of mental energy, you may not only lose their interest—you may also demotivate them.

You can also make comprehension easier by providing a familiar framework for your listener. The SoFE framework does this well by relying on beginning, middle, and end. This is a structure that everyone knows and understands well. Using one of the six story types will further increase the familiarity of your story as well.

Finally, you can employ the fourth-grader test like Bert Jacobs of Life Is Good does. It's a technique that Bert developed after seeing the success of the simplicity of the "Life is good" moniker. The test centers on whether or not a fourth grader can understand the concept or story presented. If not, it's too complicated. Bert applies this technique to every major decision the company makes: "Can a fourth grader understand it?" If there's someone in or near fourth grade in your household, you can apply the same type of test (literally) to your story. If not, I highly recommend you find a young person to run your story by. Tell it to them. If they can recite it back to you in a way that makes it clear they understood what you were telling them, then you pass. If not, you need to simplify.

UNIQUENESS

The third challenge you will undoubtedly face is the uniqueness of your idea or, rather, the lack thereof. Most founders think their business or their offering is unique, that no one is doing it quite like them. They may even be so bold as to say they have no "real" competition. The problem with this approach is that there is a high probability that someone somewhere has an offering that looks and feels exactly like theirs.

This makes it incredibly challenging for founders to figure out ways to stand out as a business because with so many new ideas constantly being put into the world, they all start sounding the same. Adding salt to your wound, you have to compete with existing product solutions that are already on the market and their brand awareness. Just head down any toothpaste, protein snack bar, or beverage aisle in the grocery store, and you will experience this firsthand.

Think of it this way: 99.9 percent of humans' DNA is exactly the same. Start-up ideas and new products are similar to this analogy in that they all feel and sound similar. If you were to hear a series of start-up pitches or founder stories all at once, the majority of them would sound like each other.

The good news is that within the 0.1 percent of DNA that isn't the same across the human race, there are three million differences between us. Your story is just like this, because your story is unique to you. Not a single person in the entire world has your story, because not one person in seven billion people has had the experiences you have. You can capitalize on the uniqueness of your story by reveling in the distinction of these millions of differences.

In chapter 5, I shared multiple ways that make a story stand out:

- Make it personal.
- Carve out a niche.
- Embrace the underdog.
- Get vulnerable.
- Count on numbers.
- Go unconventional.

As part of your review process, I want you to dive back into your story and ask yourself these questions:

- Is my story unique?
- Have I employed one or more of the methods to stand out?

If not, review these elements of chapter 5, and see how you can employ them in your story.

Make it personal. Take your audience with you in a way no one else can by capitalizing on the details, attributes, and characteristics that make this venture your very own. Within your personal experience lie the very elements that distinguish what you are doing from anyone else on this rock called Earth.

Carve out a niche. It's critical that you identify a mountain within the market landscape, plant your flag on that mountain, and claim that mountain as your own, no matter how big, small, or unknown that mountain may be. The key is to articulate that claim through your story such that your audience knows where it is and how you are going to own and defend it.

Embrace the underdog. Do not be afraid to embrace your status as an entrepreneurial underdog. Let your audience know how you are the David to the Goliaths of your industry so that they root for you and, just as importantly, they know whom to root against. Whether it's in the NCAA basketball tournament or the family with the mean sisters, we all want Cinderella to win the day.

Get vulnerable. To be vulnerable, you want to go deep and pull the layers back. When you share your business experiences, let your audience get to know who you are. Build trust and connect with your audience on multiple levels by divulging the reasons why you've put your heart and soul into your business. Uncover this burning internal drive so that your audience knows your idea is not just a crazy idea but is rooted in determination and the need to solve a real problem. Share your frustrations and provide details of how your offering is going to enhance the lives of your customers.

Count on numbers. Numbers are an incredibly powerful ingredient that can be used to enhance almost any story due to their conciseness. When you incorporate them effectively into your story, it's akin to adding a splash of color to a room—they bring it alive. Make sure the numbers are relevant to the story, are worthy of being added, and are used selectively so that they enrich the story instead of cluttering it.

Go unconventional. When you go the unconventional route, you step outside the norm and break down your audience's expectations, and they pay attention. Find ways to provide fascinating facts, extreme scenarios, or counterintuitive thoughts that surprise your audience. The introduction of something highly unexpected is a very powerful tool and can help set your story apart.

FOUNDER'S STORY: TIM WESTERGREN

When Tim Westergren graduated from college in 1988 with a bachelor's degree in political science, he didn't have a clear vision for his future. The only inkling he had as to what to do for a career was that he wanted to follow his passion—music. Tim had been playing piano since he was a child, and in college he had studied computer acoustics and recording technology at the Centre for Research in Musical Acoustics as a way to keep that flame going.

After graduation, Tim began chasing his dream. For the next ten years, he lived in a van and traveled with his band members from gig to gig while alternately working as a nanny to pay the bills. He learned the plight of the working musician by sharing highways and shows with them. Along the way, he met hundreds of artists whom he thought ought to be able to make a living as musicians but instead struggled for years and eventually left the music profession. His own band, Yellowwood Junction, never made it over the hump either.

Eventually, Tim left the traveling musician business and started writing and composing music for movies in Los Angeles. One of his primary jobs as a film composer was to figure out what the director wanted for their movie. Over time, Tim developed a makeshift methodology to pinning down the director's wants. He'd sit with the director and play a stack of CDs for them, getting the director's feedback on each song. The process did not involve specific musicological terms, as Tim would say. Instead, it was a like or dislike—essentially, a thumbs-up or thumbs-down voting process. Tim would then take the general idea of the director's likes and translate it into something musicological that he could then use to compose a new piece of music that the director would like. Tim was quite successful at this, and without even intending to, Tim realized that he'd started to create an informal genome based on musical tastes.

Right about that time, Tim read an article about singer-songwriter Aimee Mann and the trouble she was having reaching her audience. Aimee Mann's two previous records had sold more than two hundred thousand copies and received critical acclaim. But her record label did not want to release her latest album, because it wanted to focus on bigger artists who would sell in the millions instead of hundreds of thousands.

The article brought back many of the challenges and frustrations that Tim had experienced as a musician. He started thinking about the informal genome he'd created in his work as a composer and believed there might be a way to use it to solve the problem of artists reaching fans. He became determined to figure out a way to codify his musical taxonomy and marry it to mathematics to build a recommendation engine that would connect one song to another. His hope was that this would not only help consumers discover new music but also help thousands of bands get their music discovered.

In 1999, Tim got together with two other musician friends, Will Glaser and Jon Kraft, and started Savage Beast Technologies. Right about that time, the Human Genome Project was making great progress and was targeting the end of the decade to decipher mankind's genetic code. That inspired them, and they called their project the Music Genome Project (MGP). Their goal was to create a taxonomy of music so that more people could hear music similar to music they already liked. They wrote a business plan and set out to raise money.

In the first week of March 2000, they raised $1.5 million of venture capital. They set up offices and became a real start-up, packing themselves into a small studio apartment. They then hired musicians and engineers to help them create their new product. The team set out to identify the musical "genes" covering every detail of vocals, rhythm, harmony, melody, lyrics, and instrumentation. They also added a unique, high-performance algorithm that could compute the musical "distance" between songs. The music analysts they hired reviewed about ten thousand songs, one song at a time. With paper and a pencil, they slowly built their MGP database. It took them ten months to build a prototype that matched a song to other similar songs that a listener might like. They ran it inside of Microsoft Excel. Tim realized in hindsight it probably wasn't the best way to build a prototype, but it's all he could think of at the time.

To test the prototype matching engine they'd built, Tim typed in a Beatles song (either "Eleanor Rigby" or "Norwegian Wood"—he can't remember which). After a long two minutes, the matching engine came back with a song called "New York Mining Disaster 1941" by the Bee Gees. Tim immediately thought that it didn't work. After almost a year of working on the prototype and close to a million dollars spent, the engine came back with a completely off-base answer matching the Beatles to the pop band the Bee Gees. But it turns out, it actually did work.

The song that it recommended was from an earlier band with a blues sound. These Bee Gees were different from the famous pop band the Bee Gees, formed by the Gibb brothers. In fact, these Bee Gees were basically a Beatles copycat band, and their music matched well to the Beatles. Tim was ecstatic. The engine knew nothing about the metadata around these artists, but it was making musicological connections, connecting songs fairly accurately. The more they played with the prototype, the more they started believing they had an algorithm that worked. But there was one problem.

After a year of setting up the prototype and making it work, they had started to run out of money. It was 2001. They had fifty employees and cash-flow issues, and the dot-com market had crashed. Fundraising was almost impossible. Tim skipped payroll to keep the company afloat. Every two weeks, Savage Beast would hold an all-hands meeting, and Tim would beg the employees to work for another few weeks unpaid—some left, but many stayed. This went on for two years. Tim maxed out eleven credit cards, racking up debt at nearly $150,000. The company almost folded in early 2003 as former employees sued to recoup back pay, but Tim continued to work for little or no salary. Savage Beast racked up $1.5 million in back pay to employees that Tim promised to one day pay back.

At the same time, Tim continued to pitch venture capitalist after venture capitalist. But after the dot-com crash, investors were not interested in a company whose business model was still unproven and/or changing. Their business model started to morph as they considered how they could make money off the Music Genome Project. One of the first models was integrating the technology into listening kiosks in music stores. They had initial success in 2002 doing a trial in-store kiosk placement. This led to a partnership with AOL Music and Best Buy that would stretch out payments over a few years. However, that still wasn't enough capital. At that point, Tim had pitched to more than three hundred investors who all passed on the idea.

Luckily, they were able to stay alive into the beginning of 2004, despite being out of money. Tim had always found a way to infuse hope into the team, and he was able to continually craft and mold their story and vision to keep partners and outside entities inspired to do business with them. By then, he had pitched to 347 investors, trying to raise their next round of funding. In March 2004, Tim had an opportunity to pitch to Larry Marcus, a venture capitalist at Walden Venture Capital who was also a musician.

Larry loved the potential behind the genome itself and decided to invest. His firm eventually became part of a $9 million round with other investors. Tim and Savage Beast still owed about $1.5 million in back salaries to employees as well as other debts. When they finally raised that round of financing, Tim decided to surprise the employees. At the time, he had kept them fairly insulated from the process of fundraising, so no one knew that he had closed the round. At the next all-hands meeting, Tim showed up with a huge stack of envelopes. He slapped them on the table, then handed them out to the fifty employees in the room. Some people got checks for more than $100,000.

The even better news was that even though they'd lacked funding for the previous three years, they had continued growing the Genome's library. By the time they got the $9 million, the library had over seven hundred thousand songs and ten thousand artists with about ten thousand new songs being added each month. They had created a huge database and a very valuable piece of IP, or intellectual property. After they got the round of funding, they decided to sit down and think of what else they could do with it.

Despite all the changes of people, strategy, product, and story, they still had a similar mission and purpose—to introduce people to music and help musicians make a living from their music.

Larry Marcus, the lead investor, worked with them to take advantage of the IP they had built along with the music library to figure out how to migrate from a B2B model to a consumer model via personalized internet-based radio that would be ad supported.

They brought in a new CEO, Joe Kennedy, a former E-Loan and Saturn executive, and he helped develop the idea of using the music genome database as the center of an internet radio service. They got rid of the name Savage Beast and eventually came up with the name. Kennedy scribbled P-a-n-d-o-r-a on the back of a *Billboard* magazine and Pandora was born. They hired a private investigator to find the former members of a defunct band named Pandora's Box and bought the URL for $5,000. After getting all their musical ducks in a row, in September 2005 they launched Pandora.com, an online radio streaming service that allowed users to create personalized, interactive, commercial-free, dynamic online radio stations.

Today, Pandora has seventy-six million active users who listen to twenty billion hours of streaming content yearly. Pandora generates $1.5 billion in revenue annually and has paid out more than $2 billion in royalty fees to artists since they began.

RELATING TIM'S STORY TO REVIEW AND REVISE

Tim's idea for Pandora didn't come to him overnight. It was a slow burn to reach the point of success. Every part of his story had to be revised and rewritten along the way. From his start as a musician to his transition to a film composer to his start-up, Savage Beast, Tim had to learn and grow from his mistakes. He weathered the ups and downs in order to find the perfect combination of his talents and experiences. As a musician, Tim understood the struggles of finding an audience. As a film composer, Tim's job was to understand what the musical director wanted for their movie. He created an interview system that was the first iteration of "thumbs up and thumbs down." This gave him the ability to predict what directors would want, which in turn gave him the idea to codify his genomic approach to understanding musical tastes and to leverage technology to build a recommendation engine. Five years and many more mistakes and successes later, Tim finally had what we all know today as personalized radio, Pandora.

The great thing about Tim's story is that he became an expert at revisions. In the five years that Tim and his team worked to stay alive in the early 2000s, they learned what worked and what didn't. Though they had a working prototype of their initial idea, they realized they didn't have the right business model, vision, and story for what they were trying to do and continually had to revise it. Tim went through the fundraising school of hard knocks on steroids, going through three-hundred-plus investor pitches and learning from every mistake. He continually revised his pitch until he eventually landed the right investor at the right time.

One of Tim's most impressive traits is his ability to change and adapt his story over time and remain true to his vision. With Savage Beast and Pandora, Tim skillfully navigated the river of narrative change that start-ups go through when the market and business are in a state of flux. His ability to evolve helped him come up with the original idea for the company, secure the first round of funding, and survive for years through the many challenges he faced. His flexibility helped him realize that a complete business model change was needed in order to be successful. This helped him create a product that consumers fell in love with and ultimately led to a new take on the traditional over-the-air radio and broadcast industry.

I filmed Tim at a conference years ago, which featured world-class leaders building high-performing cultures, and his love of music and passion to bring his idea to life was still palpable. Tim is an authentic and sincere storyteller. His charm and charisma enable him to share his belief in the brand and vision of Pandora as a platform. No matter how many times Tim has had to rewrite the story of Pandora, one thing has remained constant. His simple goal, vision, and mission: help musicians find their audiences, and help audiences find great new music.

CHAPTER TWELVE

PRACTICING YOUR STORY

NOW THAT YOUR STORY HAS BEEN ASSEMBLED, reviewed, and revised, it's time to practice and test it. Practicing enables you to become better at delivery. If you've been doing all this work alone, this will be the first time you share your story with another, and it will help you identify the weak spots and potentially confusing areas.

Practicing, no matter who it's with or how it's done, should be a phase you spend a significant amount of time on. Don't just practice once in front of each audience—do it over and over. The more you practice, the better you'll get. When you practice your story, you start to develop a rhythm and pace that keeps things flowing smoothly. You also begin to internalize the content.

Practice is incredibly important in storytelling because of the way our brains work.

A study done by a team of integrative physiologists, published in the *Journal of Neuroscience*, discovered that the more you practice at a new skill, the less energy the brain starts to use, and it starts to focus on other things. This allows you to worry less about the content and more about delivery or interacting with your audience through eye contact or body positioning.[14]

Practice makes it easier for the brain to move data and therefore increases the efficiency and operating speed of the brain. When you practice, you physically change the brain. This gets a little bit meta, but essentially when you learn something new, you activate various portions of the brain. When you present your story in front of an audience, for instance, the brain coordinates a complex set of actions that involve audio and visual processing, verbal language skills, and even our motor functions. Initially, your story will feel unnatural, awkward, and stiff.

The more you practice something, the more natural it becomes. The process will feel smoother because you'll start to memorize the content and develop your flow in the delivery, and it will become second nature to you. Instead of sounding like you're repeating what you've

14   Helen J. Huang, Rodger Kram, and Alaa A. Ahmed, "Reduction of Metabolic Cost during Motor Learning of Arm Reaching Dynamics," *Journal of Neuroscience* 32, no. 6 (2012): 2182–90, DOI: https://doi.org/10.1523/JNEUROSCI.4003-11.2012.

memorized word for word, it'll sound like you're naturally sharing an experience.

As you practice, I highly recommend you study some of the great storytellers who have been referenced in this book: Howard Schultz from Starbucks, Sara Blakely from Spanx, Scott Harrison from Charity: Water, Tony Robbins, and many more. Go online and find their videos. Watch how they tell their story. Visit the Storytelling for Entrepreneurs website, and study our stories and analyses of these famous founders. Your story is going to live with you for the life of your company and beyond; this investment in practicing is worth the time, energy, and emotional output. When you practice, your story becomes a natural extension of your being because you no longer have to worry about memorizing what you are saying and how you are saying it; now you are simply sharing a part of you. Through practice, you can reach that level where your story becomes the entrepreneur's Swiss Army knife that can help you accomplish all your business needs.

There are three audiences I recommend you practice with. The first is yourself, the second is your family and friends— those closest to you—and the third is your professional network—colleagues, mentors, and fellow entrepreneurs.

PRACTICE WITH YOURSELF

We often discount how good we are at being able to give ourselves feedback. We are all great critics because we constantly make decisions about what we're going to give our attention to in this world, and we've developed filters that help us discern what is great quality and what is bad.

There are three highly effective ways that you can practice with yourself. First, I want you to read your story aloud and listen intently to how it sounds. Is there emotion? Inflection? Does it make you interested, or are you bored? You want your story to feel conversational. If you were to read a job description aloud, it would sound like a job description. Your story should not sound like a job description. It should draw you in, be compelling, and strike an emotional chord in your audience.

One of the things that might be helpful during this practicing phase is to record yourself as you're reading aloud. This can be audio or video or both. Each one will allow you to listen to how the story sounds, and video will help you see how you look. I know...it's awkward to see yourself on camera. Very few people like to see themselves onscreen, but when you video yourself, you will find all the little nuances that happen while telling your story that may or may not be beneficial.

When you record your story, you can work on timing.

Many people think their story is sixty seconds long, but when they record themselves they find that it takes three to four minutes and never realized it. Recording your story is a great way to edit and revise your story as a listener versus the teller. When you play back the audio or video recording, you can make notes or changes on the written version of your story like an editor would.

The more you practice and review, the more you can create different lengths of your story so that you'll be prepared for any situation or medium. Often, our stories end up in print on a website or in an email we send, and you want to make sure that a reader understands what you're saying and is interested.

FRIENDS AND FAMILY

The second audience that you want to utilize is your friends and family. These should be people who are rooting for you to succeed and are willing to take the time and energy to help you with your story. This time should be used for you to observe their responses and put in your practice time so that the telling of your story continues to become more natural. I highly recommend you do this in person, but if you need to do it over the phone or record it and email it to someone, that will work, too, as long as they're willing to follow up and give you feedback.

I like to think of this as the safe space to practice. While it's great to practice in front of others, the probability that you are going to be given a realistic perspective from this group is very low. Most of the time, friends and family won't give you the true, unfiltered feedback that you need to improve your story. This is because they are going to give a biased opinion in your favor for most things that you do, or they may not tell you what they really think since they are close to you. However, you should still practice with them because they'll support you regardless, and that support will give you the confidence to keep going. Also, you may get lucky and have some friends and family who will give great honest feedback. They may find all kinds of problems with your story or even think it's not a good story—that can be invaluable at this stage even if you don't agree with what they are saying. It's good practice to go through this process and hear the responses, good or bad. At this point, any feedback you receive will be beneficial.

YOUR PROFESSIONAL TRIBE

The third group you want to practice with is your professional tribe. Your professional tribe is typically your close-knit business network that is generally supportive but is also a little detached and able to give you feedback that is the closest to what the real world thinks. These people are probably fellow business owners, mentors, advisors, and business partners. For those who are or have been founders, there is a very good chance that they have probably had experience with their own story. When you tap into these professional colleagues and peers, they can give you constructive feedback because they've most likely been in your same situation. They can tell you what happened to them and how to avoid certain pitfalls, or they can give you advice on what worked for them.

While this audience will be the closest to reality, you still want to keep in mind that the feedback you get most likely will not represent the exact feedback, or lack thereof, that you'll get from audiences you ultimately want to share your story with, such as investors, journalists, and customers.

HOW TO ASK FOR FEEDBACK

Rather than simply sharing your story and saying, "Hey, give me some feedback," I recommend you have five questions ready for your test audiences so that you can get structured responses that are helpful. These five questions will help you elicit specific feedback.

1. What was the best part of the story and why?

Generally, you're looking to see if they found the hook or that memorable aspect of the story that you wanted them to walk away with. You will also quickly find out whether you obtained and kept their attention.

2. What was the weakest part of the story and why?

Here you're looking to see if there's something that doesn't work or isn't strong enough to be included.

3. Would you share this story with someone else? Why or why not?

This is a test to determine whether your story is compelling and engaging enough that they'll want to share it with others. Within their answers you will also be able to judge a certain level of enthusiasm. If they excitedly tell you they know exactly who they're going to go share your story with, then you're right on track. If they say, "Yeah, I'd share it," but don't seem that enthused, then you might want to consider revising your story to make it more compelling. Consider what would make them more enthusiastic about sharing it, or even press them as to why they might not share it. That kind of digging can give you some valuable insight to figure out ways to make your story more captivating.

4. Can you repeat it back to me?

Not everyone will want to do this, but if they can tell you

a short version of your story, then you know you've made it memorable. Their ability to articulate the story back to you is a direct reflection on your ability to tell it. If they're able to articulate your story accurately, that's a good litmus test for you to determine whether your story was effective, compelling, and memorable. If they have trouble, then you must decide whether it was something you did wrong or maybe they just weren't paying attention. Either way, you're going to gain valuable information on the impact and memorability of your story and their ability to repeat it back to you.

5. How does it make you feel and why?

This comes back to your story goal. Remember, the goal of the story is not the business need. The goal of the story is to leave your audience with a specific feeling. If the feeling they repeat back to you after you ask them this question is in line with the feeling you wanted to leave them with, then you've accomplished the goal of your story.

USING THE FEEDBACK

As you go through this process and receive feedback, I want you to remember what my mom, Eva Graft (Mother G), says: "Listen to everything I have to say, take what you need, and throw away the rest." Take all this feedback with a grain of salt, because everyone will have an opinion. There is a good chance you will get different feedback from different people. Some of the feedback will not be helpful, and some will be illuminating. Evaluate the feedback and modify as you go.

I encourage you to apply that same philosophy when you're listening to all this feedback, because if you truly believe in what you're doing, you're going to keep working on this idea regardless of what people say. However, be open to their feedback. Listen and take it sincerely. Focus on the critical feedback that truly feels like it is going to improve your story. If you keep hearing the same thing over and over, yet you don't necessarily agree with it or aren't sure how to act on it, then seek out someone to help you. This may be one of those situations where you need to gather a team of folks to have a kind of "story intervention" where they discuss your story in a group—debating what works and what doesn't. Use that feedback to help you evaluate and modify your story as you go. The more you share your story, the more you're going to know how effective it is and the better that story will become.

TESTING YOUR STORY

After you've practiced your story, you need to test it in a live-fire environment. The difference between testing and practicing is that practice has no real risk. You practice with people who know and care for you and want to see you succeed. When you test your story, there is some level of risk. The investor could say no; the customer could pass up your offer. When you introduce risk to your story, you create pressure. Pressure is one of those things in life that you don't know how you are going to respond to unless you experience it firsthand. The good thing about situations where there will be pressure is that they force you to be better prepared because now there are consequences for sharing your story. When you practice and test with pressure, over time you will get better, and it will get easier.

When you go live with your story, I recommend starting with low-risk environments. Professional comedians do this often. Instead of going out on the road when they have new material, they'll try it out at a local club or an open mic night. They don't book an entire tour until they've practiced and tested their material.

You can do the same thing by working with local and regional events in your area. You can speak to universities and high schools. Almost every city has some type of networking event or Meetup gathering relative to a business area or field that would love to have you speak to their group. Instead of trying to reach out to *USA Today*, maybe there's a local or neighborhood newspaper that you can share your idea or story with.

Next time you get invited to a meeting and you have to go around the room and introduce yourself, use that sixty seconds to tell a brief version of your story. Often, you will find that if you make a positive impression, people will come up to you afterward and ask to know more or ask for your help.

In these live-fire environments, you can utilize these low-risk opportunities to see how people respond. Do they respond in a way that meets your business needs? Do they write about you in the local paper? Like the comedian testing material, did you get a laugh when you shared that joke? Did someone come up to you after the meeting and ask to know more? Or ask if you needed an investor? These questions and scenarios are all great ways to identify if your story is working in the way you want it to.

These are also times that you can get feedback as well. If you have the time and your audience permits it, you can ask the same five questions you asked audiences earlier. If during the testing process you notice that your audience looks at you with dumbfounded looks or asks you a million questions afterward, or no questions at all, that is an indication that your story is unclear. At this point, it would be wise to reevaluate your story and see where you can simplify or replace certain things to make the entirety more interesting.

In the case of FindMyFourLegger.com, if I noticed the

audience was tuning out or confused, I would revise accordingly. It might be the case that they want to know more about the product. In this instance, I would add that the device attached to the collar glows in the dark so that the dog is more visible at night. Or I might explain that it works like Find My iPhone. If people were tuning out early on, I might spend more time explaining why my dog is so important to me at the beginning of the story.

When you revise, it is up to you to decipher the feedback, then think about ways you can make your story more compelling. Does the incident grab the audience's attention? Are you sharing enough obstacles so that the audience understands how much you went through? Is the outcome powerful enough that they feel they need your product or service? Does it make them want to share it with someone else?

Another way to test your story that mimics reality is to migrate between different media. Let's say you meet with someone and share your story in person. As you return to revise it, I want you to try a different medium, whether that's writing it down or filming it. In the real world, you often won't have a choice on how your story is delivered. You could meet an investor in an elevator, you might be interviewed on a local news station, or you might have to write it in an email to send to a prospective client. In any case, it's best to be prepared to present it in any medium.

The more you practice moving from medium to medium, the more effective you will be at telling your story in any situation. For example, let's say you've been working on your story in Microsoft Word and you feel it's strong. However, two days later, you find yourself on the subway with someone you've been wanting to get in touch with for five months. You should be prepared to tell them your story without having to have a document or device in front of you. Being prepared to share your story on any medium and practicing it consistently will set you up for success.

FOUNDER'S STORY: MARC BENIOFF

Marc Benioff, founder of Salesforce.com, changed an entire industry based on a vision of how enterprise software needed to change. As part of his process to make this vision a reality, he practiced and tested ideas and stories long before he put them to use because he knew they would be integral to his success.

Marc had been working for Oracle, one of the most successful enterprise software companies in history, and was one of their top salespeople, yet he was no longer motivated or inspired. So he asked his boss, the founder Larry Ellison, if he could go on a mini sabbatical. After a decade working for the company with such success, Larry granted him the request. Marc took a six-month break and went on a global quest to rediscover his passion. He rented a beach hut on the Big Island of Hawaii, explored the Arabian Sea in rice boats, and traveled to India, where he met the Dalai Lama. One of his good friends, Arjun Gupta, who was starting a company in Silicon Valley, came with him on the trip to India.

During this trip, they stumbled upon a little hut in a city called Trivandrum. There they met Mata Amritananda-mayi, more affectionately known as the hugging saint. They sat with Mata in meditative sessions, letting her know that they were on a quest. They were both at a time in their lives when they were looking for more. They confessed their lives, talking about their anxieties and fears as well as their hopes and dreams. Arjun even took out his business plan for a venture capital firm and started reading it to the saint. He talked about the future of technology and mobile going to the cloud and connectivity. The guru Mata patiently sat listening to Arjun for an hour, then turned to him and said, "While you are working so hard to change the world and do all these great things, don't forget to do something for others."

As Marc listened to the guru talk to Arjun, he felt as if she were talking to him. It occurred to him that he didn't have to make a choice between doing business and doing good. That sparked an idea in Marc that maybe there was a different approach to enterprise software. An idea that would show itself somehow in the coming months. The next day, Marc and Arjun returned home to the United States. Arjun went on to start his VC firm, and Marc returned to his office at Oracle.

Back at Oracle, Marc received what he calls a "fateful call." He was asked to attend the President's Summit for America's Future as a representative of Oracle. At the conference, U.S. General Colin Powell gave an inspiring speech about giving back to the communities and the youth. The speech ended with, "Just remember this. Get out there and do something for other people." For Marc, that speech was another epiphany. He felt as if Colin Powell was echoing the words he had heard from Mata. Upon returning to Oracle, he talked to his boss, Larry Ellison, about creating a foundation. Larry agreed to the plan, and Marc put it in motion. In the daytime, he would build products and services for the clients of Oracle. In the nights and mornings, he would help put computers in schools, train teachers how to use them effectively, and work with kids.

Marc's foundation was off to a great start. He even received a call from General Powell himself. The general had adopted MacFarland Middle School in Washington, DC, and Marc and his team were needed to install computers. On an extremely hot day in DC, Marc and his team of three engineers headed over to the school to install the computers with the help of other Oracle team members. However, they ran into a problem. There was no one to help them carry the computers up the three flights of stairs to the computer lab. It was the end of the quarter, and none of the Oracle employees had shown up because they had to focus on hitting their sales numbers. The task was impossible. Marc called General Powell and told him they would have to reschedule—he didn't have the manpower to complete the job. Marc apologized profusely, but the phone went dead. The general had hung up on him. Marc felt terrible.

A bit later, the phone rang. It was Marc's lead engineer. A battalion of marines had shown up at the middle school, and they were installing all the computers. Though the project turned out to be a success, Marc felt as if he had let the general down because Oracle's employees had not shown up. He sat at his desk feeling dejected. Maybe he had gotten the whole thing wrong. Maybe trying to do all these altruistic things along with business and technology was impossible.

Marc learned something that day. If you are going to connect your business and your philanthropy, then you need to integrate that philanthropy deep into your culture. It can't simply be tacked on. In that moment, Marc knew it was time to leave Oracle and launch his own business. Marc quit his job, rented an apartment in San Francisco, and started working on his mission. Heavily influenced by his time in India and his sabbatical from Oracle, he knew he needed a different kind of approach for how technology, and specifically software, was done. And he wanted to build a company from the ground up that integrated a culture of giving.

He came up with the idea of how to build his new company in his sleep. He had a weird dream where he envisioned Amazon.com, but instead of tabs with Books, CDS, DVDS, and so on, they said Accounts, Contact, Opportunities, Forecasts, and Reports. That morning, he woke with the words of Walt Disney in his head: "If you can dream it, you can do it." Though he had no idea how he was going to do it, he knew his mission had been set.

Marc had an idea for an approach to enterprise software that would be different—inexpensive, easy to use, and accessible from anywhere in the world. He declared war against the traditional way software was sold and delivered to companies and began his mission to provide a better way to serve technology customers.

He started making big statements about taking on huge established companies such as Siebel Systems and even Oracle. Publicly, he defined his mission for his start-up to be "The End of Software." Everyone thought he would crash, but he pushed forward, creating a logo and slogan for "No Software" similar to the *Ghostbusters* movie logo. He even made the phone number for the company sales line 1-800-NO-SOFTWARE.

Marc constantly tested his ideas with friends, the press, and customers so that he could learn what resonated with them and what didn't. He'd invite friends and colleagues over to his apartment, which was the headquarters for his start-up, which he called Salesforce, to try out the software and provide unfettered feedback on what they liked and hated. Testing his ideas allowed him to constantly fine-tune his message and selling points.

On July 21, 1999, the *Wall Street Journal* ran a front-page story called "Canceled Programs: Software Is Becoming an Online Service, Shaking Up an Entire Industry." The article spoke about the software-as-a-service concept and generated more than five hundred leads even though the launch was still six months away. Other publications picked up on "the end of software as we know it" theme and ran follow-up articles.[15] His company had traction because of practice and constant testing of his ideas. It's what enabled him to get Fortune 500 companies to sign up for his software as a service before the product even

15   Marc Benioff and Carlye Adler, *Behind the Cloud: The Untold Story of How Salesforce.com Went from Idea to Billion-Dollar Company-and Revolutionized an Industry* (San Francisco: Jossey-Bass, 2009).

existed. That product would become known as Salesforce. com.

Today, Salesforce has thirteen thousand employees and $5 billion in revenue. Keeping with the lessons he learned from Mata and General Powell, Marc decided to create a radically different philanthropy that was integrated into Salesforce from day one. He called it the 1-1-1. Salesforce would forever be committed to putting 1 percent of their equity, 1 percent of their profit, and 1 percent of their employees' time into a 501(c) public charity. Their efforts have received accolades from *Fortune* and *Forbes* magazines and have given $50 million to charity.

Marc's style and story are great to study because beyond his ability to test and practice his ideas, one of the biggest reasons Marc's methods worked was the grandeur of the idea Marc put out there. It was borderline outlandish that he would make claims such as "the end of software," and it led to a ton of free publicity. He also played the underdog card. His company was the David, and the other established industry leaders such as Siebel Systems were the Goliaths. He turned the giants' strengths against themselves and used his small size and upstart nature as compelling advantages. Of course, this approach is not for everyone, but every entrepreneur can steal a little bit of Marc's bravado, because you are going to need some of that as you take on the real world.

CHAPTER THIRTEEN

_____

OWN YOUR STORY

NOW THAT YOU'VE PRACTICED YOUR STORY AND are prepared to share your creation with the world in a live-fire environment, there are a few things I want to leave you with.

First, let me say: doubt right now is normal. You might be thinking, is story really all that and a bag of chips? Is it as powerful as this book makes it out to be? Are people really going to want to hear my story? And will it help me as a founder to be more successful in business?

As someone who drinks as much storytelling Kool-Aid as I do, I still encounter doubt every once in a while. Each time I catch myself wondering if all this story work is worth it, I remind myself of a little experiment that writer/brand analyst Joshua Glenn and *New York Times* contributor Rob Walker conducted, called Significant Objects.

Joshua and Rob had a hypothesis:

"Narrative transforms insignificant objects into significant ones."

They believed that "stories are such a powerful driver of emotional value that their effect on any given object's subjective value can actually be measured objectively."[16] To test this belief, they created an experiment. Their idea was to have a talented writer invent a story about an everyday object and see if that story added value to the object. They believed that "invested with new significance by this fiction, the object should—according to our hypothesis—acquire not merely subjective but objective value. How to test our theory? Via eBay!"

To prove their theory, they purchased one hundred objects from thrift stores and garage sales for a total cost of $128.74. They then hired writers to create fictional short stories for each object, and placed them for sale on eBay. After the stories were complete, they posted the items with the fictional stories on eBay with a disclaimer that the stories were purely fiction. They took care in making sure that eBay customers would not feel as if this was some sort of hoax, so they included the author's byline with the story. This ensured that whoever saw the listing

---

16 "About the Significant Objects Project," Significant Objects, accessed November 12, 2018, http://significantobjects.com/about/.

would know that it was not a true story. When the sale was complete, they mailed the "significant object," along with a printout of the object's fictional story. The authors retained all rights to their stories, and net proceeds from the sale were given to the respective author. Here is a partial example of one of the items posted along with its story:

ITEM: PEPPER SHAKER
COST: $0.99
EBAY DESCRIPTION STORY

Lily hesitates before the open door of the empty pantry. Alone on one of the shelves sits a silvery white saltshaker, seemingly the only thing left behind by whoever once lived in this small house. Lily's finger follows the puncture marks of the S that stretches across the top, and she imagines the tiny awl, the steady hand, the tap of the hammer. She shakes it, but no grains rattle inside. When she begins to twist off the top, a faint metallic scrape of the threads stops her, as if the sound were some warning. She places the shaker back on its shelf...[17]

The story goes on to show Lily imagining taking a journey on a boat to search for the lost companion of this salt shaker. It touches on the themes of seeking balance

<hr />

17   Philip Graham, "Pepper Shaker," Significant Objects, January 14, 2010, http://significantobjects.com/2010/01/14/pepper-shaker/.

in the world—finding someone who completes us—and finding our own way home. After reading the story about that pepper shaker, everyone's mind was abuzz.

The ninety-nine-cent pepper shaker sold for twenty-eight dollars.

That's how powerful the story was.

At the end of the project, all hundred objects were sold, for a total of $3,612.51. Adding stories to these seemingly "worthless" items yielded a twenty-eight-fold return. To be sure their hypothesis was correct, Joshua and Rob repeated the study years later, with similar results. Their hypothesis had been proven correct once again: adding story increases value. This is one of the primary reasons I wrote this book—to help you leverage the power of story on your entrepreneurial pursuit. Your story will add value.

FIND THE BELIEVERS

This Significant Objects experiment brings home the next thing I want to leave you with, and that is to seek the right audience.

One of the reasons that eBay itself was so successful is that it demonstrated that there is a market for just about every kind of object on the planet—no matter how obscure or valuable.

You can sell practically anything on eBay, because someone somewhere wants that item (for the right price). eBay made it possible for an eBay seller to find the audience that wants the item.

As a founder, you need to find the people who want what you are offering. Over and over, I've seen entrepreneurs try to pitch their idea or product to everyone they encounter. They believe everyone will love what they have to offer, but life and reality do not work like that. Not everyone will like what you offer, just as not everyone will want that salt shaker from eBay.

Your job, then, is not to worry about convincing the masses that your idea or product is what they need or want. There will always be naysayers and nonbelievers, and you will constantly run into them. They will ignore you for reasons beyond your control. I don't care who you are or what your product or service does; there will always be someone who will happily point out the negatives. Focus on those looking for the Kool-Aid you are selling. If you're selling iced tea, find the people who are thirsty. Don't try to sell ice in the Arctic or pitch space heaters in the desert.

Don't spend your energy and emotions going after everyone. Instead, channel your efforts toward the believers. Find the people who are interested in supporting what you do, and go after them. They are the ones your story is going to resonate with the most.

OWN IT

My final thought, and the most important thing you need to do when you are done with your story, is to own it completely.

This sounds intuitive enough, but its power became incredibly clear to me when I spent three days with John Paul DeJoria, founder of Paul Mitchell hair-care products, while we were developing the pilot for the TV show that would eventually go on to become the primetime CNBC series we created and produced, called *American Made*. The revelation I had during my time with John Paul was so profound that it has become a fundamental element to my teaching and coaching entrepreneurial storytelling.

Here is that story.

FOUNDER'S STORY: JOHN PAUL DEJORIA

In 2006, I had my first opportunity to create a pilot for a television series. In order to create a pilot for an hour-long TV show about entrepreneurs, we had to find a high-profile founder who would be willing to let us figure out how to create this show from scratch. Luckily, a friend introduced us to billionaire John Paul DeJoria, and John Paul allowed us into his life for three days to capture his story for the pilot episode. Having access to a well-known entrepreneur didn't mean we'd immediately be able to produce a television show, but we were lucky with John Paul, because his story exemplified the American entrepreneurial dream, and his compelling backstory gave us a strong foundation to start with.

John Paul's parents divorced when he was two years old. He lived with his mom in East Los Angeles in a constant state of poverty. By the age of nine or ten, he was selling Christmas cards door to door and delivering newspapers to help the family make ends meet. By the age of twelve, his mother could no longer support him. He found himself living in a foster home and eventually joined an LA street gang. Luckily, he didn't stay in the gang long, and he joined the navy. When he got out of the navy, he worked a variety of jobs selling products door to door—from cleaning supplies to encyclopedias. Eventually, he landed in the beauty industry because he believed he could make a name for himself selling beauty products.

In his sales positions, he was doing well. However, his success threatened others, and he ended up getting fired from three different companies he had been working in sales for. During these challenging times, he often found himself homeless, living in his car, or sleeping on a friend's couch, all while taking care of his three-year-old son. He'd even go to certain restaurants during happy hour, order water, and tip the waitress a dollar, so he could get free food from their complimentary buffet.

Despite all these setbacks, John Paul knew he was a good salesman and had great ideas. Eventually, he teamed up with a man by the name of Paul Mitchell, who was a chemist.

Together, they created a shampoo-and-conditioner product combo they believed was better than anything on the market and would be easier to sell. They found an investor to back them for $500,000 to launch the company, but at the last minute the investor backed out. At that point, John Paul had already made a number of commitments, and he was determined to launch the company regardless. To do this, he had to think fast. He was able to cut out, drastically reduce, or simply delay almost all of the expenses. Unfortunately, the designer who did all the artwork would not accept a payment plan, so John Paul and his partner, Paul, scraped together the only money they had left—$700—to help pay the artist for the logo on the bottle design. Because color printing was too expensive, the logo became black and white. John Paul convinced everyone else to let him pay in two weeks to thirty days, and started selling his first hair-care product out of the back of his car, one hair-care salon at a time.

That first year, they made more than a million dollars. Today, their company, now called John Paul Mitchell Systems, is worth more than a billion dollars and is one of the most well-known hair-care brands in the world. And that black-and-white color has become an iconic style statement in the industry.

As I listened to John Paul, over those three days I was fascinated by his life's story, but more than that, I wanted to understand what made John Paul's telling of his story so compelling. The details about his life made for a great story, but he wasn't an eloquent speaker like Howard Schultz, he didn't have the emotional appeal of Scott Harrison, nor did he necessarily have the same incredible passionate delivery as Tony Robbins.

John Paul had something else.

It was something I'd seen many times before, yet I'd never been able to pinpoint it. Because of the skills the other successful entrepreneurs had in telling their stories, it hadn't been so obvious. They were captivating because they were great orators or they simply told their story incredibly well. John Paul had me intrigued for another reason. Now it was clear.

John Paul truly owned his story. That was what made him so compelling. It was more than him simply being a good salesperson, of which there is no doubt. He unabashedly believed what he was saying.

I've been around plenty of people who sell their products, but John Paul DeJoria was different. He was not schlepping products or blowing smoke about how good they were. He had conviction. He honestly believed without reservation that his products were going to make your life better. When John Paul DeJoria told people about Paul Mitchell, he believed that a small dollop of his shampoo in your hand would improve your life, because your hair would look and feel better and be easier to manage. When he talked about pouring from that beautiful Patrón bottle, he believed life would be better because you'd be drinking one of the most sophisticated and high-quality tequilas in all of Mexico, enjoying life to the fullest.

It didn't matter that he wasn't a gifted orator because he grew up in the streets, or wasn't a great storyteller because he was better at sales; he truly believed his products would improve your life, solve your problems, and make everything better. He had complete conviction and ownership over his story, and that compels people to buy his products or be part of what he is doing.

As an entrepreneur, you need to approach your story in

the same way. If you want people to be compelled, you must own your story with total conviction, regardless of where you are in the business timeline. If you don't own your story, no one else will. Conviction and belief is truly contagious. When you tell your story with that reverence, that enthusiasm, that passion, people will start to say, "I don't know what it is they're on, but I want whatever it is!"

I could write an entire book about how to do just that—in fact, I will—but for now, you are more than ready. It's time to tell your story.

CONCLUSION

WHEN I STARTED GIVING SPEECHES TO ENTREPRE-
neurs and corporations, I would search for powerful
quotes to leave my audiences with at the end of my sessions. I wanted to impress upon them the lasting impact
a story could make. This is the quote I share the most:

> Tell me a fact and I'll learn. Tell me a truth and I'll believe.
> But tell me a story and it will live in my heart forever.
> (Indian Proverb)

I share it with you now for that same reason. What I've
learned and experienced hundreds, if not thousands, of
times is that a great story can touch the deepest part of
one's soul and leave an indelible mark in the mind. All of
us remember stories we've heard throughout our lives—
stories that are deeply implanted in our memories for
years to come.

What's unique to you as an entrepreneur is your heartfelt life experience that led to the creation of your business. You have now learned to craft a story that not only has the potential to be a lasting and impactful memory you leave your audiences with, but it can also convince them to help you get what you need as a founder.

Because you are a founder, you are going to be given an endless supply of opportunities to tell your story in an incredibly diverse number of settings and circumstances, from the time you launch your start-up through the entire life of your company and beyond.

At every networking event you attend, in every pitch you make, in every email you send, you are given a moment to speak from your soapbox.

To share your story.

How you manage those encounters—whether they're thirty seconds, three minutes, or half an hour—can be pivotal to the life and success of your company.

You have to have the best founder's story possible because you never know if this is the right time, the right place, or the right person who could lead to the sale, the introduction, the investment, or the article that catapults you to greatness.

Everything I've covered in this book, and everything you've done so far, has been to prepare you for these moments. Embrace them.

This Swiss Army knife of entrepreneurship that is your story is going to be your lever that you use in almost every critical situation you face as a founder. It is the one thing that celebrates what is unique about you and your offering, while building that emotional bridge to get your audience to take an action that supports your cause.

As an entrepreneur, you have chosen to commit to something greater than yourself, to bring a vision to life that is going to transform the lives of others forever. You have an unshakeable desire to do something unforgettable, and you want your story to light them up.

So take stock in every goosebump experience, aha moment, or gut-wrenching memory that is a story waiting to be crafted by you through everything learned over the last thirteen chapters.

This is your time to leverage your story to help you get what you need to build an amazing business.

Own this time. Make a permanent mark.

Most stories end here. But for your story, this is just the beginning.

And that's the best part.

ACKNOWLEDGMENTS OF AN AUTHOR'S JOURNEY

THE STORY OF THE BOOK

YEARS BEFORE I STARTED WRITING THIS BOOK, I was in an introspective period, trying to find my calling. I was running a successful video production company but knew that I had not landed on what I was meant to do. I loved capturing and sharing inspiring entrepreneurial stories and producing videos, and although I was gifted at it, my gut and soul were nagging at me to do more.

During this period, the idea about writing a book started out the way it does for many authors—people telling you that you should write a book about everything you have been doing for the last decade. For me, that meant writing all that I'd learned from filming and sharing the stories of entrepreneurs. At this point, the book was still just an idea on the future to-do list.

THE ONE THING

Then, in 2012, I was filming an entrepreneur conference and got to meet and film one of the keynote speakers of the event, Gary Keller, the founder of Keller Williams Realty.

As someone who films founders for a living, few talks knock me off my feet anymore. This night was different. Gary was different. What he said, how he said it, where we were, and more importantly, where I was in the search for my calling were all in sync.

Gary had just finished writing his book with Jay Papasan, *The ONE Thing*, and it was a focal point of his keynote. He started out by sharing his journey into real estate right out of college and how a major setback had slapped him in the financial face like only a "real estate deal gone wrong" can do. He immediately started dropping huge pearls of wisdom gained from this setback and proceeded to flood us with invaluable advice with story after story.

I bought Gary's book the next day and began internalizing what Gary had opined the night before—the core premise of his book: "What's the ONE Thing you can do such that by doing it everything else will be easier or unnecessary?"

I started to contemplate the "one thing" that I could do to help me on my quest. And I would dedicate the first hour of every day to doing it.

Then the idea returned...I was focused on how writing a book would allow me to get my ideas, thoughts, and knowledge on paper and help me better understand what I was meant to do. I realized writing a book could be a catalyst for all the ideas that were percolating in my head. Maybe this was the path to my calling?

FORTY DAYS

The idea stayed with me for weeks, but I didn't act on it. Then one night, I sat across from my best friend, Ingrid Vanderveldt, over dinner and told her what I was thinking. I also shared with her that it was time for her to write the book she had always talked about, and shared my "one thing" enthusiasm.

Something struck a chord in her, and over the next two weekends, she spoke thirteen chapters into a microphone over thirty hours and had a draft of a book. I was so incredibly proud of her, and also taken aback by how quickly she had done it. An insatiable fire lit inside me.

I began thinking about how I might go about the process

of actually writing my own book, but I wasn't sure exactly how to start.

Right about that time, my friend Erin Fall Haskell, who was working on her doctorate in mediation, posted about doing a forty-day commitment to bring about change in your life.

Simultaneously, another friend shared a story with me about taking a forty-day spiritual journey and how the number forty was a revered number in history and in a variety of religions.

I could sense the universe was telling me something—now it was just a matter of time.

DAY ONE

You know how it is sometimes...One day you wake up and decide to do something and you actually do it.

For me, it was Friday, February 1, 2013, when my journey began. I decided to commit to spending the first hour of every day for the next forty days working on a book (whatever that meant, since I actually had no idea how to write one).

I grabbed a blank piece of paper and my producer clipboard, then I stared writing and drawing. I'd segment words, phrases, and headers and then go back and circle, underline, and tag the best stuff. Then I typed those items into my computer and made a one-page table of contents.

Day one complete. Day two was spent taking that one-pager from the day before and expanding one of the chapters into its own outline. Each day was similar in that every day thereafter would involve fleshing out a section, bouncing around from the beginning to the middle to tangents but always making progress on something.

There wasn't much rhyme or rhythm to it; it just kind of came out. And I wasn't quite sure if there was a book there or not, but it felt good to pour myself into the process for the first hour of every day. I could feel the progress I was making on something I had only thought about for years.

At the twenty-day mark, I noticed subtle feelings of doubt and frustration creep in—you know, the kind that kick in on really big projects. This was when I was most vulnerable to stopping the writing process. Trepidation arose on whether I could turn these outlines and scribbles into an actual book. But I was committed to forty, so I plowed through it and kept going.

Then it happened. On the thirty-first day out of forty, I saw the book unfold before me, and I knew it was exactly what I needed to be doing. The vision was incredibly clear. My mind, body, and spirit aligned. I needed to go in the direction of this book, and that is what would lead me to a clearer interpretation of my calling. I needed to write and finish this book.

After the euphoria of my "aha moment" passed, the reality of writing a "real" book set in, as did the fact that I still didn't know what I was doing. Onward I went—working on it every day—sometimes one hour and other days six hours, depending on my mood, workload, and inspirations. Oddly, I loved and cherished that part of the process. It turned out to be my saving grace because I had no idea how long the journey would be...

I'm forever indebted to Gary, Ingrid, and Erin, as they were true catalysts for getting me on the horse to start to write this book in the early days. Funny thing is, those days turned into months, and months into years, and six years later the book is finally ready.

SEA OF GRATITUDE

This is where a sea of gratitude and appreciation comes in for all those that were part of it.

If not for them, I'm not sure this book would ever be in your hands.

Let's start from the top.

To the most important woman on this planet, my mom, Mother G. You are my North Star in life—providing more inspiration, joy, and warmth than I can ever explain. A constant stream of optimism, pride, encouragement, and love that has gotten me through everything in life, and especially this book, even though you never knew it. Your stories have been a staple of my world, and having you as a mother is the greatest gift I've ever been given. And I adore having you as my number one fan (as evidenced by your liking every post I've made on social media). If anyone is ready for this book to come out, it's you. Thank you for everything, especially your love.

To my sisters, Cindy, Lindy, Mindy, and Windy, for being the foundation of my life. It was you four incredible women who taught me kindness, giving, love, and laughter. Few things compare to sitting around the dinner table, lounging next to a roaring fire, or hanging out on the backyard deck with you all—drinking Palomas and eating home-cooked New Mexican food—all while sharing nonstop stories and laughing for hours on end. That continues to be one of my favorite pastimes. It's from you and Mother G that I learned the storytelling craft, because it is all that we do.

To my BFF, Ingrid Vanderveldt, one of the brightest

lights on this planet, filled with compassion, caring, and authenticity. Thank you for always being there for me in the good times and the challenging moments, supplying your unending source of positivity and optimism, and forever being that person I could confide in. I'm constantly humbled by your ability always to see the good in me and make me feel as if I was the best in the world at this and that I was truly meant to do this. I am beyond blessed to have you be part of my life.

To my four-legged best friend, Fitty G. You showed me why dogs are called man's best friend. You are an unwavering silent supporter as my coauthor, as you've been by my side the entire writing trip and beyond. Helping me understand the meaning of unconditional love every single day has carried me through this journey as if the universe placed you there for this very purpose. I owe you everything and cherish every moment with you—even when you steal my burritos from the coffee table when I'm not looking.

To my trusted longtime assistant and writing sensei, Brett Randell. Having someone who writes for a living be just a text, email, phone call, or pizza-and-beer gathering away while writing a book was an author's creature comfort I'll always remember. A "Jack and Coke" toast to you.

To my longtime production partner, Toby Schwartz,

founder of Real Normal Productions. Few things compare to having an incredibly talented producer and writer as a sounding board and good friend when it comes to checking your work, giving you ideas, and trusting someone to give you frank, unfiltered feedback. Every content creator needs a Toby in their life.

To my New Mexico brethren from undergrad: Jon Stanford, TA Corcoran, Scott Harenberg, Dino Pellicano (and Willy Melfi), who have been with me through thick and thin since back in the day. Luckily, we are all still alive. My storytelling chops were groomed in the halls of our old house and continue thanks to our road trips and gatherings. I feel blessed that we are still telling stories and making memories after all these years. I'm honored to call you my extended kin—forged through the experiences of life and the bonds of doing some really cool (and dumb) things together.

To my Texas Longhorn brothers from other mothers, Mike Appel, Tom Inman, Wes Breyfogle, and Paul Shaffer, for always making it about getting together and enjoying the splendor of life. It's hard to describe how important these gatherings have been to me, having friends who don't ask about or really know about what you are doing but support you regardless. It's only that we gather, laugh, and live out loud for as long as this world will have us.

And thank you to Amy Cosper for the editor-in-chief

writing tips, Dr. Paul Zak for the neuroscience lessons, Erin "Jonesie" Jones for her creative prowess, and Jared Tennant for the MacGyver tech support. Your support was more important than you realize.

THANKS FOR RITUALS

What was really fascinating about the book-writing process was all the rituals and places I found myself incorporating into my daily routine, which have become a part of this book. Each day I'd wake up at 5:00 a.m. or so, lie in bed until my mind kicked in fully (typically about thirty minutes), write for sixty to seventy-five minutes, and then take a break to head over with Fitty G to my favorite healthy food truck of all time, Picnik, founded by Naomi Seifter. I'd have a green matcha butter latte with brain octane and discuss the day with the workers and patrons before heading back to start the rest of the day.

Along the way, I got introduced to the beauty, elegance, and challenge of yoga by a chance filming of the founder of Wanderlust Austin, Ashley Spence. I decided to do another forty-day challenge to experience yoga "proper like" by going to her studio and taking a one-hour yoga basics class. Three years later and I'm still going two to three times per week, as yoga has become part of my life. And surprisingly, yoga became a grounding effect for me writing the book. It reminded me of my days as a snow-ski instructor and math tutor, when I approached teaching with a "beginner's mind" to better relate to my students. That novice perspective has been invaluable in crafting the SoFE framework for the book, course, and teachings.

ALONG COMES A SCRIBE

After a few years of working on the book solo-style, I started to look at various options to get the book published. I talked to other authors, researched independent book publishers, and attended conferences and events to learn about the process. By then, I was knee-deep in writing daily, building this war chest of entrepreneurial storytelling research, founder profiles, lessons, and knowledge that was supposed to somehow fit into a book.

This is where Scribe comes in (called Book In a Box at the time). A friend introduced me to the founder, Tucker Max, right before he and Zach Obront started the company. I ended up producing videos for Scribe and got to interview twelve-plus authors, hearing firsthand how Scribe had made an incredible difference in their own books and even their lives. As I look back, I bought into the concept immediately, but it took me a while to get out of my own way and drop the ego and let them help me. It was one of the best decisions I've made because it has allowed me not only to get the book done but to begin to focus on the larger picture of the Storytelling for Entrepreneurs platform.

To Tucker, I owe you a massive debt of gratitude for your unfiltered feedback on that chapter I tried to do on my own, by letting me know I really did need help. But even more so for becoming a great friend along the way, providing invaluable advice as well as a place to go when I needed it.

To Zach, for getting the process started and making sure I was beyond satisfied at every step. To Hal Clifford, for helping me transition from video producer to author by introducing me to the book outlining process. To my ever-patient publishing manager, Emily Gindlesparger, for ushering me along through all the moving parts of the book. Your graceful acceptance of life getting in the way yet delicate prodding of me to keep the ball moving is appreciated more than you know. And especially to my writing muse who helped me find my voice, my editor, Cory Martin. Scribe is not about ghost writing or writing for you. They are about taking the ideas that are in your head and the words that you speak and turning them into book prose that becomes the paragraphs on these pages. It's an amazing process, and Cory has been my trusty Sherpa all along the way—giving me guidance, freedom, and sage counsel through it all. I'm forever in her debt for her patience, support, and belief.

And to JT McCormick, Scribe's CEO and foundational rock. I'll never forget the phone call I got from him when I was going through a particularly hard time in my life, saying, "Don't worry about a thing. We'll be here for you. Just keep doing what you do. 'We' got this." I cannot thank the entire Scribe team enough. I'd probably still be treating the book-writing process as if I was trying to write my opus if it wasn't for the team at Scribe. Instead, I know this is the first of more books to come.

STANDING IN GRATITUDE

When I started writing the book, I had no idea it would take as long as it did or that so many layers of myself and my purpose would unfold as they did.

Along the way, there have been countless others who have all played special parts in my own personal narrative and who helped stoke the writing fire in their own unique way.

First and foremost, the entrepreneurs and founders in this book. Thank you for being the men and women in the arena "whose face is marred by dust and sweat and blood; who strives valiantly," as Teddy Roosevelt so eloquently stated in his famous speech. Your passion, commitment, and willingness to dare greatly constantly fuel my drive, and those features are why I love sharing your stories.

Strangers I met who expressed their belief that countless aspiring founders would benefit from what I was doing and that it was sorely needed. Professional peers who thought I just wanted the author title or that I naively believed it would bring me success. Baristas who wondered what it was like to pour your heart into something on a daily basis. Authors I connected with who looked down upon me as though I saw too much promise in my pursuit or who felt I had no idea what I was doing (partially true on the latter—thank goodness for Scribe!). Members of audiences I spoke to who came up to me after my talk asking how they could get their hands on the book as soon as it was ready. Clients who inquired as to when I'd actually be done with this book, wondering if it would ever get released—in a loving way, of course. Colleagues who were dismissive, as they saw it as another frivolous entrepreneurial pursuit after all these years. And friends who offered unwavering support because they truly wanted me to shine brightly for others and share my gift with the world.

Thank you. All of you.

Each of you played a special part in the creation of this book, and for that, I'll forever be grateful.

For me, this writing was never about the book or being an author. It was about what I would discover on the journey. It was about the mental and emotional ride I knew I would go through trying to get my ideas out to the world, and how that voyage would hopefully illuminate the road I needed to be on. It was all that and so much more, as that path is clear to me now.

But I must say, it feels fabulous to have this book completed, and I might even add "author" to my title for certain introductions. I didn't realize how much of an impact this book would have on me, how humbled I would be by those who made it possible, and how much it would mean to be able to share it with you.

Lastly, thanks to you, the reader, as you are now part of my journey. I'm incredibly honored that you invested the time to read this book and learn about what I wanted to share. For that, founder to founder, I thank you.

In gratitude,

Lyn Graft

ENDNOTES

FOUNDER'S STORY REFERENCES

MARC BENIOFF

Marc Benioff and Carlye Adler, *Behind the Cloud: The Untold Story of How Salesforce.com Went from Idea to Billion-Dollar Company and Revolutionized an Industry* (San Francisco: Jossey-Bass, 2009).

"A Conversation with Marc Benioff, Founder & CEO of Salesforce.com [Video, Transcript]," Endeavor, February 16, 2012, http://www.endeavor.org/blog/marc-benioff-keynote/.

University of Southern California, *Marc Benioff USC Commencement Speech | USC Commencement 2014*, YouTube video, May 16, 2014, https://www.youtube.com/watch?v=YFEgzfb_LBY.

University of California Berkley, *Marc Benioff Speaks at UC Berkeley Commencement*, YouTube video, May 18, 2015, https://www.youtube.com/watch?v=nEJpq16mP6g.

"How to Pursue Innovation with Marc Benioff," Salesforce Work.com Blog, October 2013, http://work.com/blog/2013/10/pursue-innovation-marc-benioff/.

David A. Kaplan, "SalesForce's Happy Workforce," *Fortune*, January 19, 2012, http://fortune.com/2012/01/19/salesforces-happy-workforce/.

"Storytelling Tips from SalesForce's Marc Benioff," *Businessweek*, November 2009, http://www.businessweek.com/smallbiz/content/nov2009/sb2009112_279472.htm.

Chris Preimesberger, "Marc Benioff: Trend Seer and Business Socialist," *eWeek*, May 19, 2011, http://www.eweek.com/c/a/Cloud-Computing/Marc-Benioff-Trend-Seer-and-Business-Socialist-257483/.

JEFF BEZOS

J. R. MacGregor, *Jeff Bezos: The Force Behind the Brand: Insight and Analysis into the Life and Accomplishments of the Richest Man on the Planet*, Kindle edition (Sheridan, WY: CAC Publishing, 2018).

Amazon.com Full Story—World Biggest Online Retailer Revealed, YouTube video, September 2013, https://www. youtube.com/watch?v=smygeWmpavA.

Chuck Severance, *Jeff Bezos 1997 Interview*, YouTube video, December 22, 2013, https://www.youtube.com/ watch?v=rWRbTnE1PEM.

Corporate Valley, *Amazing Amazon Story—Jeff Bezos Full Speech*, YouTube video, May 27, 2013, https://www.youtube. com/watch?v=YlgkfOr_GLY.

Chip Bayers, "The Inner Bezos," *Wired*, March 1, 1999, http://archive.wired.com/wired/archive/7.03/bezos_pr.html.

Eric Jackson, "6 Things Jeff Bezos Knew Back in 1997 That Made Amazon a Gorilla," *Forbes*, November 16, 2011, http:// www.forbes.com/sites/ericjackson/2011/11/16/6-things-jeff- bezos-knew-back-in-1997-that-made-amazon-a-gorilla/.

Richard L. Brandt, "Birth of a Salesman," *Wall Street Journal*, October 15, 2011, https://www.wsj.com/articles/SB10001424 052970203914304576627102996831200.

Brad Stone, "Jeff Bezos and the Age of Amazon," *Business Week*, October 10, 2013, http://www.businessweek.com/ articles/2013-10-10/jeff-bezos-and-the-age-of-amazon- excerpt-from-the-everything-store-by-brad-stone#p1.

Rob Walker, "Jeff Bezos, Amazon.com," *Inc.*, January 4, 2004, http://www.inc.com/magazine/20040401/25bezos. html.

"Jeff Bezos," Academy of Achievement, 2013, http://www. achievement.org/autodoc/page/bez0bio-1.

SARA BLAKELY

Spanx, *Sara Blakely of SPANX Speaks at The Edge Connection— Atlanta, GA*, YouTube video, September 9, 2011, http://www. youtube.com/watch?v=m1tTZSuHJKM.

Conn Jackson, *Sara Blakely: How She Started Spanx*, YouTube video, January 6, 2012, http://www.youtube.com/ watch?v=kFx-RdVLheI.

"How Spanx Got Started," *Inc.*, online video, accessed November 12, 2018, http://www.inc.com/sara-blakely/how-sara-blakley-started-spanx.html.

"'My Own Butt' Spanx Inspiration: Billionaire Inventor," CNBC, October 16, 2013, http://www.cnbc.com/ id/101116826.

Teri Evans, "Sara Blakely on Resilience," *Entrepreneur*, March 21, 2011, http://www.entrepreneur.com/ article/219367.

"Success Stories: Sara Blakely," SUCCESS, http://www.success.com/article/success-stories-sara-blakely.

Claire O'Connor, "How Sara Blakely of Spanx Turned $5,000 into $1 Billion," *Forbes*, March 14, 2012, http://www.forbes.com/global/2012/0326/billionaires-12-feature-united-states-spanx-sara-blakely-american-booty.html.

ADAM BRAUN

Adam Braun, *The Promise of a Pencil: How an Ordinary Person Can Create Extraordinary Change*, Kindle edition (New York: Scribner, 2014).

Adam Braun, *Adam Braun: How He Started Pencils of Promise*, YouTube video, 2014, http://www.youtube.com/watch?v=EV2KSKbob_8.

Journey of Action, *Adam Braun's Inspiration for Pencils of Promise*, YouTube video, 2011, http://www.youtube.com/watch?v=JdAM-MUjhNo.

David D. Burstein, "Innovation Agents: Adam Braun, Justin Bieber, and Pencils of Promise," *Fast Company*, May 2012, http://www.fastcompany.com/1835510/innovation-agents-adam-braun-justin-bieber-and-pencils-promise.

Shirley Halperin, "Adam Braun on Pencils of Promise and How Justin Bieber Is 'Making the World Better,'" *Hollywood Reporter*, July 28, 2011, http://www.hollywoodreporter.com/news/adam-braun-pencils-promise-how-216267.

Rebecca Serle, "The New Nonprofit: Pencils of Promise," *Huffington Post*, November 29, 2010, http://www.huffingtonpost.com/rebecca-serle/the-new-nonprofit-pencils_b_785603.html.

Dan Schawbel, "Adam Braun—How He Started Pencils of Promise," *Forbes*, March 18, 2014, http://www.forbes.com/sites/danschawbel/2014/03/18/adam-braun-how-he-started-pencils-of-promise/.

Catherine Clifford, "Pencils of Promise Is Giving Nonprofits a Hard-Nosed Entrepreneurial Facelift," *Entrepreneur*, November 26, 2013, http://www.entrepreneur.com/article/230126.

Anne Vandermey, "Why You Should Ditch Your Desk Job," *Fortune*, March 17, 2014, http://management.fortune.cnn.com/2014/03/17/adam-braun-pencils-of-promise/.

"Adam Braun on His New Book, Surviving a Near-Death Experience + Justin Bieber as a Role Model," MTV, March 18, 2014, http://act.mtv.com/posts/adam-braun-the-promise-of-a-pencil/.

Helaina Hovitz, "Pencils of Promise Founder Reminds Us to Focus on the Children, Not Just the Statistics," *Huffington Post*, March 7, 2014, http://www.huffingtonpost.com/helaina-hovitz/pencils-of-promise-founde_b_4922056.html.

MICHAEL DUBIN

Dollar Shave Club, *Our Blades Are F***ing Great*, YouTube video transcript, March 6, 2012, https://www.youtube.com/watch?v=ZUG9qYTJMsI.

Dollar Shave Club Website, accessed November 12, 2018, http://www.dollarshaveclub.com.

Benjamin F. Kuo, "Interview with Michael Dubin, Founder of Dollar Shave Club," socalTECH, March 22, 2012, http://www.socaltech.com/interview_with_michael_dubin_dollar_shave_club/s-0041685.html.

Darren Dahl, "Dollar Shave Club, From Viral Video to Real Business," *New York Times*, April 11, 2013, http://www.nytimes.com/2013/04/11/business/smallbusiness/dollar-shave-club-from-viral-video-to-real-business.html?pagewanted=all&_r=0.

Ashley Vance, "Dollar Shave Club's Founder: 'Yes, I Am a Funny Guy,'" *Businessweek*, March 12, 2012, http://www.businessweek.com/articles/2012-03-12/dollar-shave-clubs-founder-yes-i-am-a-funny-guy.

Nate C. Hindman, "Michael Dubin, Dollar Shave Club: Razors 4 Less," *Huffington Post*, March 8, 2012, http://www.huffingtonpost.com/2012/03/08/dollar-shave-club_n_1326884.html.

Katie Morell, "Michael Dubin: The Terrible Part about Having a Viral Video," American Express Open Forum, February 25, 2013, https://www.openforum.com/articles/building-an-empire-michael-dubin-of-dollar-shave-club/.

Emily Glazer, "A David and Gillette Story," *Wall Street Journal*, March 12, 2012, https://www.wsj.com/articles/SB10001424052702303624004577338103789934144.

Jack Neff, "How Dollar Shave Club Hit a 'Nerve Center' with Consumers," *Ad Age*, July 3, 2012, http://adage.com/article/cmo-interviews/questions-razor-marketer-ad-age-cmo-strategy-summit-speaker-michael-dubin/235750/.

Jessica Naziri, "Dollar Shave Club Co-Founder Michael Dubin Had a Smooth Transition," *Los Angeles Times*, August 16, 2013, http://articles.latimes.com/2013/aug/16/business/la-fi-himi-dubin-20130818.

J. J. Colao, "Dollar Shave Club: Breaking the Razor Blade Monopoly," *Forbes*, April 3, 2012, http:// www.forbes.com/sites/jjcolao/2012/04/03/ dollar-shave-club-breaking-the-razor-blade-monopoly/.

TONY HORTON

Mark Dietel, *Tony Horton Summit 2012*, YouTube video, June 25, 2012, http://www.youtube.com/watch?v=LPq-Rj-4NpM.

Wall Street Journal, *P90X Fitness Series Creator Tony Horton— WSJ Interview*, YouTube video, February 10, 2012, https:// www.youtube.com/watch?v=gCXAXDu29Uk.

Angela Haupt, "Tony Horton, P90X Creator, on What He Eats for Breakfast and How Yoga Saved His Life," *Huffington Post*, September 12, 2013, http://www. huffingtonpost.com/2013/09/12/tony-horton-p90x-yoga-breakfast_n_3902266.html.

Eric Adelson, "P90X Factor: The Childhood Secret to Fitness Guru Tony Horton's Success," *ThePostGame*, October 6, 2011, http://www. thepostgame.com/blog/eye-performance/201110/ p90x-factor-secret-tony-hortons-success.

Dina Spector, "Paul Ryan Can Thank This 54-Year-Old Man for His Ripped Body," *Business Insider*, September 27, 2012, http://www.businessinsider.com/tony-horton-p90x-inventor-paul-ryan-fitness-2012-9.

Stuart Pfeifer, "Tony Horton: Personal Trainer to the Masses, *Los Angeles Times*, January 1, 2012, http://articles.latimes.com/2012/jan/01/business/la-fi-himi-horton-20120101.

Burt Helm, "The 22nd Time Is the Charm," *Inc.*, June 28, 2012, http://www.inc.com/magazine/201207/burt-helm/how-i-did-it-carl-daikeler-beachbody.html.

Amy Levin-Epstein, "P90x Creator Tony Horton: My Success Secrets," *CBS News*, June 14, 2011, http://www.cbsnews.com/news/p90x-creator-tony-horton-my-success-secrets/.

Carol Bardelli, "Fitness Trainer of the Stars: Tony Horton Biography," *HealthyNewAge*, http://www.healthynewage.com/blog/p90x-fitness-exercise-program/.

BEN SILBERMANN

Ben Silbermann, *Co-founder of Pinterest Shares His Story*, online video, http://cofounder.tv/videos/ben-silbermann-cofounder-pinterest-story/.

Startup Grind, *Ben Silbermann (Pinterest)—The Early Days of Pinterest*, 2012, YouTube video, http://www.youtube.com/watch?v=oZYYzoSugfE.

Startup Grind, *Ben Silbermann (Pinterest)—His Background*, 2012, YouTube video, http://www.youtube.com/watch?v=P_-_JxymBTg.

Pinterest Business, *Pinterest Co-Founder and CEO Ben Silbermann*, 2013, YouTube video, http://www.youtube.com/watch?v=KwligCoQUAo.

Tomio Geron, "Ben Silbermann on How Pinterest Slowly Grew to Massive Scale," *Forbes*, October 22, 2012, http://www.forbes.com/sites/tomiogeron/2012/10/22/ben-silbermann-on-how-pinterest-slowly-grew-to-massive-scale/.

Christine Lagorio-Chafkin, "Introducing the 2 Young Men Who Made Pinterest," *Inc.*, July 12, 2012, http://www.inc.com/30under30/christine-lagorio/ben-silbermann-evan-sharp-founders-pinterest.html.

Alyson Shontell, "Meet Ben Silberman, the Brilliant Young Co-Founder of Pinterest," *Business Insider*, March 13, 2012, http://www.businessinsider.com/pinterest-2012-3.

Sara Wilson, "Ben Silbermann, Pinterest Founder and CEO, Talks Criticism and Fears," *Huffington Post*, November 27, 2012, http://www.huffingtonpost.com/2012/11/27/ben-silbermann-pinterest_n_2173143.html.

Bryan Keplesky, "Pinterest's Ben Silbermann to 'Treps: Make Something Beautiful," *Entrepreneur*, March 14, 2012, http://www.entrepreneur.com/blog/223155.

Carole Cadwalladr, "Ben Silbermann—The Modest Genius Behind Pinterest," *The Guardian*, April 5, 2014, http://www.theguardian.com/technology/2014/apr/05/pinterest-interview-ben-silbermann-social-media.

Tom Simonite, "Pinterest's Founder: Algorithms Don't Know What You Want," *MIT Technology Review*, February 9, 2013, http://www.technologyreview.com/qa/511096/pinterests-founder-algorithms-dont-know-what-you-want/.

Jessi Hempel, "Is Pinterest the Next Facebook?" *Fortune*, March 22, 2012, http://fortune.com/2012/03/22/is-pinterest-the-next-facebook/.

Max Chafkin, "Can Ben Silbermann Turn Pinterest into the World's Greatest Shopfront?" *Fast Company*, August 30, 2012, http://www.fastcodesign.com/1670681/ben-silbermann-pinterest.

ABOUT THE AUTHOR

LYN GRAFT is the founder of Storytelling for Entrepreneurs, an online platform for founders to help create, tell, and share their story. Over the last fifteen years, Lyn has filmed and captured the stories of more than five hundred of the world's top entrepreneurs, including the founders of LinkedIn, Starbucks, Dell, and Whole Foods. He has produced more than eight hundred videos focused on entrepreneurs, start-ups, and business content and dedicated twenty thousand hours to studying and practicing entrepreneurial storytelling. Lyn is an entrepreneur, producer, dog lover, and co-creator of CNBC's *American Made*. He holds a BS in electrical engineering from New Mexico State University and an MBA from the University of Texas at Austin.

Made in the USA
Middletown, DE
27 February 2019